D0715882

I Will
Walk
Alone

Ciarán McCarthy

Ballpoint Press

Published in 2016 by Ballpoint Press
4 Wyndham Park, Bray, Co Wicklow, Republic of Ireland.
Telephone: 00353 86 821 7631
Email: ballpointpress1@gmail.com
Web: www.ballpointpress.ie

ISBN 978-0-9954793-0-2

While every effort has been made to ensure the accuracy of
all information contained in this book, neither the author
nor the publisher accepts liability for any errors or omissions made.

Book design and production by Joe Coyle at Síniú Meáin & Dearadh,
joecoyledesign@gmail.com

© Cover photography by Gráinne Jordan.
Inside photography from Ciarán McCarthy's personal collection

Printed and bound by GraphyCems

Contents

Foreword

Ollie Campbell
Former Ireland and Lions outhalf

S OMETIMES when I think of Ciarán McCarthy I think of that colossal and regal seated statue of Abraham Lincoln in Washington DC.

Abraham Lincoln is the most written about, most studied and most revered president in American history and like him Ciarán has the quality of never giving up and never accepting defeat.

Lincoln once said "to remain as I am is impossible, I must improve or die". As far as I am aware, Ciarán has never said these words but he most certainly has lived them, on a daily basis, since his catastrophic injury on January 27th, 2002.

It is said that hope is the pillar that holds up the world and Ciarán has never given up hope since that day, despite the many setbacks and the many hurdles he has had to overcome.

Another man I sometimes think of when I think of Ciarán is Richie McCaw, the All Black double World Cup-winning captain who once said that in his life he has no rear view mirror. Ciarán has that same philosophy and only ever seems to think about the future, and what yet might be.

Before every game he played, McCaw wrote notes for himself in his notebook which was an on-going working document throughout his playing career. For McCaw, if it wasn't written down it wasn't real.

Like McCaw, Ciarán had to get his thoughts down on paper too. It is a real life, poignant story that is written by a genuine, honest, courageous and truly heroic human being and this book gives an insight into his life so far and his many outstanding and inspiring personal qualities will be confirmed by anyone who reads it.

Like Ciarán himself, it is a rare gem.

*I dedicate this book to my family for providing me
with the best support system I could wish for*

Introduction

MY mother was absolutely adamant, 'do not walk into any puddles'. I was disappointed, reminding my mother that I had my 'wellies' on so I would be completely dry if I did splash into puddles and besides granddad would make sure that I stayed dry. Mother was not convinced that granddad would be as responsible as she expected him to be and she was right. I went outside holding my granddad's hand and once the front door was closed he whispered in my ear that we would splash in as many puddles as we could.

I was delighted as we headed down the fields and actively sought out every sodden patch of ground we could find. Once a puddle was found a splash soon followed. The more I splashed the more my granddad encouraged me to continue. I was delighted with myself; disobedience created a heightened state of elation and utter joy. We eventually found our way back to the house and much to my mother's chagrin but not great surprise I was soaked to the skin.

While this, my earliest memory, involves waterlogged fields and an associated feeling of great excitement; a more recent memory also involves excess water and fields, but lacks that same joyous feeling.

It had been raining heavily overnight and the pitch was not in a very playable condition.

One

A Big Splash

IT was November and the 'All Blacks' were on tour. Ireland were due to play them in the afternoon but before that fixture came another match the Irish Bar Vs the Northern Irish Bar or a bunch of Dublin barristers against a bunch of Belfast barristers. I had been asked to guest on the Dublin team. Not having played in over 10 years, I was curious to see how it would go. It went well. We won and I felt more than satisfied with myself. That single match reminded me of how much I had missed playing the game. Soon afterwards a barrister asked me if I would be interested in playing for a junior club in Terenure. I jumped at the chance.

I joined CYM Terenure in early December 2001. CYM were in danger of dropping to a lower division and had a few vital matches upcoming in the month of January. One of those matches was to be played away from home in Edenderry. The match date was Sunday, January 27, a date that I will never forget.

I got up early that day. It was much like any other Sunday morning with my younger brother completely 'flat-out' asleep after a night on the town. My grandfather was also asleep though not as a result of a night out. More as a consequence of his 96 years than anything else. My parents unlike the other two were awake and enjoying a little treat I prepared for them each Sunday – their breakfast in bed.

I drove down to the club and decided since I was not familiar with Edenderry's grounds I would travel by coach and leave the car parked in Terenure. After a 90-minute journey we arrived in Edenderry. It had been raining heavily overnight and the pitch was not in a very playable condition. Apparently drainage had been an ongoing problem for Edenderry Rugby Club for many years.

Since we had arrived well in advance of the kick-off we took the opportunity to travel into the town for something to eat. Having sated ourselves we returned to the grounds. As we trooped into the dressing room the groundsman was forking the ground to remove some of the surface water but I put the weather conditions out of my head and concentrated on the more usual pre-match routine.

The dressing room was spartan in that it was small, bereft of heat and in dire need of a face lift. In other words no different from most other changing rooms at this level of purely amateur sport. Each player tended to hog whatever space he could find and claim it as his own by spreading out the contents of his bag as widely as possible, thereby maximising space to the detriment of those around them. Not exactly a sharing and caring thing to do but nonetheless practised widely and consistently. We sat there and tried to focus on the game.

There was pre-match tension in the air, a tension that finds different outlets of expression in each player. Some players were absolutely silent. Others needed to talk, talk about anything just as long as they could hear their own voice. Some chose to use liniment, some stretched, others stayed still, all just willing the time to pass until it was 30 minutes before kick-off. At that point, all the players put their playing gear on, each with an individual number on their back and with different roles to play within the team yet prepared to play together as a single unit. To me, my teammates were mostly strangers as I had only just returned to the game.

About 20 minutes into the game I was tackled and felt winded but continued to play. Then about 10 minutes later I noticed one of their players was fringing around a maul. This maul like any other in rugby was a loose collection of opposing players attempting to secure possession of the ball.

Occasionally, a player will sneak the ball away from the melee and go on a plundering march up-field towards the opposition's goal line. That is what was about to happen. The small crowd sensing this let out a roar and being close to both sets of supporters, it was a noise that was ringing in my ears as I met his charge with one of my own. He was marauding forward in a straight line with his legs pumping, the surface water splashing and mud smeared across every inch of his body. The mud was so thick that the colour of his jersey was barely visible.

I intended to drive my right shoulder directly into his left thigh by diving directly into him from the side. I charged towards him and was about to dive towards his targeted leg with my body weight propelling me forward. My arms were out in front of me and about to wrap themselves around his legs when the soft ground went from under me.

Thus, all propulsion was gone. My shoulder and head bounced off his thigh and my arms flailed about in their futile attempt to grip his legs. I hadn't managed to bring him to the ground. Instead I fell backwards with my skull and backside crash-landing on the freezing, sloppy mud. After a moment of passing disorientation, I realised he too was about to stumble primarily because the ground was more liquid than solid.

I tried to roll away from under his feet but I could not. I was stuck in the mud, sitting up trying in vain to wriggle my feet away from the wet suction of the oozing turf. His feet gave way and he fell directly onto my upper back forcing my torso down towards my knees. That was when I felt and heard a cracking sound coming from my back. Within seconds of this first cracking sound came a second. I was in deep trouble. The maul had collapsed and two more bodies fell in on top of us. This second cracking sound was instantly accompanied by sensation and movement draining down my body and out my toes. My legs had become numb and immobile.

I had an idea that work probably was a non-starter the next day ... but what would the day after that bring?

Two

A Horizontal
Viewpoint

A S I lay on the hospital trolley on that early Sunday evening my head began to race. One of the first thoughts to pop into my head was; no work tomorrow, when could I go back? Managing a legal publications company for me meant getting up early heading into town for a 7.30am start and finishing in the afternoon. I had an idea that work probably was a non-starter the next day but what would the day after that bring? Where would I be? How would I get there? How bad was this injury? All I knew was I certainly didn't want to be laid out flat, looking up at a ceiling just waiting for a doctor to give a diagnosis.

Two contrasting voices started to resonate throughout my head. To me, these voices represented Fear of paralysis and Faith in recovery. Fear spoke first and Faith replied:

'You are damaged, you are broken everything is changed; changed utterly.'

'I may be physically damaged but now is the time for courage and I will show it.'

'Wonderful sentiment. However there is no denying the reality of immobility.'

'Not yet, but with time I will heal.'

'Perhaps. Of course it's not just your legs that are problematic you can not feel anything from your belly-button down.'

'I have always been a good healer and this is no different.'

'No different, are you sure of that? After all what organs will be affected?'

'What organs are situated in that part of the body? I can think of three: intestines, bladder and gonads.'

My internalised conversation was interrupted by a doctor. He placed one X-ray after another onto a bright screen and began to talk.

'We have the results of your X-rays and scans. It's not good. You have broken your back.'

There was a slight pause in the young doctor's speech, just a short period when no words were uttered and yet it was the most revealing point in the conversation. This was when fear was temporarily displaced by powerlessness and panic. Feelings that made the drab accident and emergency department grow to monstrous dimensions. In that moment I had in my own mind become less significant to the life I had been leading. It was a situation that seemed to be getting worse with each passing second.

'Yes it is worse, you have sustained a spinal cord injury.'

'But I feel numbness in my legs. Surely any feeling is good news?'

'The numbness in this instance is not good.'

'How long will it take for this paralysis to go? A week, a month, a year or longer.'

'There is no way of telling. Recovery if it comes at all, varies from patient to patient. I have worked with spinal cord patients before in Sydney. Some recover completely but others do not. How heavy are you?'

My reaction to the question was delayed, with my mind racing and muddled I could not think properly. Then it struck me, why did he ask that question? Here I was with one half of my body dead and the doctor wanted to know my weight.

'... we need to prepare a steroid bolus and to give you the right amount, we need to know your body weight. It will prevent further destruction of your tissue at the area of injury.'

I gave my weight but this conversation was not helping me. All I could now think of was it's bad, it's bad, it's bad. Somebody else approached the trolley. It was the president of the rugby club. He, at least temporarily, brought me out of my stupor.

'I think it's time you told your family what happened.'

With that he handed me his mobile phone. The news I had to deliver was of the most unwanted, unwelcome and shockingly destructive variety. The tranquility and laziness of a Sunday afternoon at home was obliterated without trace.

'Hello Mom, it's me.'

'When will you be coming home?'

'I won't be home tonight. I've been injured in the match and I'm at Tullamore Hospital.'

My mother's voice started to waver, 'What happened?'

'I broke my back. It's a spinal cord injury.'

'... what are the doctors saying?'

'The registrar on call said recovery varies in degree from patient to patient. At best no one knows whether I will walk again...'

That was the hammer blow and it felt to me like I was the one holding the hammer. At the same time, I knew now was the time to be strong. Even though that inner voice was shouting; 'your life is over you may as well be dead. This is the first day of a battle that may go on for many years.'

Added to her wavering and pausing was my mom's determination not to cry on the other end of the telephone. I knew it was only a matter of time before her emotional turmoil would be too much to control, so it was time to end the call.

I had woken up that day, got out of bed, gone downstairs, had breakfast and driven to the club; all ordinary activities. Eventually repeating such simple activities in the same way would be extraordinary given my current state. I knew this was true as did those close to me.

The night before the operation, my immediate family, with the exception of my grandfather, was called into the hospital to speak to the surgeon and his team.

Three

Medicine

S TEROIDS were given to me four hours after the injury took place. Their purpose was to prevent further destruction of the cord. Had I gone to another hospital such treatment may not have been forthcoming. In short the greater the necrosis or destruction, the greater the likelihood of a 'complete' cord injury. A 'complete' cord injury is a trans-section or severing of the cord – it leaves no prospect of ever walking again. Given the nature and position of my injury an operation to stabilise my spine was essential. Without it a 'complete' cord injury would ensue.

The operation was carried out at The Mater Hospital in Dublin. The journey to Dublin took place soon after 7 o'clock in the evening; it was a quick trip due to the special Garda escort. On both journeys to the hospitals I had difficulty breathing. It was not until the next day that I found out why. Once I was assessed by the doctors on call that night in the Mater it was decided to operate on me the next morning.

It was described as being a stabilisation operation with metal rods and bolts being inserted above and below the level of the injury. During the course of the operation the tackle I received prior to the spinal injury came back to haunt me. As it turned out it resulted in fractured ribs puncturing my right lung leading to a pneumo-thorax. This resulted in my lung capacity or capacity to breath being diminished. That was an unwelcome complication for the surgical team. I did not return to the intensive care of the national spinal unit until late afternoon having been sent to surgery in the early morning.

The night before the operation, my immediate family, with the exception of my grandfather, was called into the hospital to speak to the surgeon and his team. My father is the consummate family man, in that he is selfless, his energies and efforts are both focused and directed for the benefit of his family. My mother is another selfless person and like my dad is in her early seventies. She too puts her family ahead of herself.

I have two brothers, one lives in Italy and to a great extent was spared the initial emotional assault of a brutal diagnosis. The other brother is six years my junior and has a child-like enthusiasm for life that few of us manage to retain, that is, if we ever experience it in the first instance. My immediate family was shown to a private room away from any prying ears. The surgeon, my surgeon, to whom they spoke is a man with over 30 years experience and unsurprisingly is well respected within the upper echelons of Irish medicine.

'The situation is as serious as it can be. Your son has sustained a burst T12 fracture. He has a 'complete' injury and is paralysed from the waist down. The injury is more akin to a horse riding accident than it is to a rugby accident.'

'Is the spinal cord severed?' he was asked.

'No. It is not. However the damage is so severe that it is akin to a total trans-section or severing.'

'Do you think he will walk again?'

'He has slim to no chance.'

'When you say slim. What does he need to do in order to walk?'

'To walk he will have to lift and bend his legs at the knees.'

'What about his bladder and so on?'

'He will have bladder, bowel and sexual dysfunction. However medical intervention in each case is possible.'

'Have you ever come across people who have managed a return to full health after such an injury?'

'It is not unheard of, but it is unusual. I have been in medicine long enough to know that miracles do happen.'

Once a week the rehabilitation consultant from Dun Laoghaire paid me a visit in the spinal unit of the Mater Hospital. He, like my surgeon, was a man of great experience and at that stage was not far away from retirement.

He didn't sugar-coat his remarks.

'I have spoken to your surgeon and reviewed your chart. You're a paraplegic but you will retain independence. That's a blunt statement, do you have anything to say?'

'Yes, I do have something to say. Is it possible for you to definitively rule out any future improvement?' I asked.

'No,' he answered.

'That is due to the nature of the condition. Is it not?' I probed further.

'Yes.'

It wasn't a pleasant exchange for me and from his demeanour I suspect he was irritated by my questioning. But I wanted answers even if they stopped him somewhat in his tracks.

It would be a full month before I would get to the rehabilitation hospital. Steroid treatment and the stabilisation operation were important changes in circumstance but once in 'rehab', there would be a third change in circumstance: physiotherapy on a daily and intense basis. After a full month in bed I was prepared to begin my time in 'rehab'.

The day of the operation had been the day I was to go on a blind date with the housemate of my cousin. Needless to say that particular rendezvous never took place.

Four

A New Friend And Slow Progression

S OON after my first contact with the rehabilitation consultant I found my faith in recovery was being challenged by my fear of paralysis.

'You will retain your independence, who is he fooling? This same man who called you a paraplegic,' said Fear

'So paraplegics lack independence?' asked Faith.

'They would have to be more dependent on others after their injury than before it.'

'This you hold true in every instance?'

'You know that universal statements tend to be general in nature rather than specific.'

'I do know. Just as I know to assume truth from a position of ignorance, is all too often, inaccurate.'

'There are times when I am accurate.'

'And there are times when you are not.'

The day of the operation had been the day I was to go on a blind date with the housemate of my cousin. Needless to say that particular rendezvous never took place, however within days of the incident I had a visit from both my cousin and her flatmate.

There seemed to be a spark between us, but it was only over time that what we shared became clearer. After receiving a single red rose with a best wishes card on Valentine's Day, I thought that the attraction I felt towards this woman might mirror her attraction to me, yet I had a doubt. About a week later this strikingly tall dark-haired woman with brown eyes walked into the ward and started to tell me how nervous she was about coming into the hospital.

'I wasn't sure what to wear.'

'You came, that is the only thing that matters.'

'Yes, but I wanted to get my hair, make-up, clothes, everything right.'

I leaned towards her and kissed her gently. A new romance had just begun and there I was lying in bed with tubes attached to my nose and arms while completely dependent on a mechanised bed just to turn over.

On Tuesday of the second week in hospital, the president of the rugby club came into the ward and asked me my view on what happened leading up to and including the incident on the field. He asked, 'Where do you apportion blame? If anywhere.'

'I blame the conditions.'

'I'm meeting with the club's ruling committee on Thursday night to formally agree a report that will be sent on to the IRFU (the Irish Rugby Football Union). The referee made it clear should the conditions get any worse then the match would be suspended but as things stood the pitch was playable.'

The following week the president of the club returned with a somewhat different emphasis. He thought that the game should have been cancelled not due to playing conditions but because of the fact that the club could not put out its strongest side and were not in a position to be competitive at all.

This viewpoint was not something I lent great credence to. The president went on to say that I was covered by an IRFU insurance policy and the club had its own insurance cover for its members.

My parents and brother were daily visitors to the Mater Hospital. Of the three my mother was the strongest perhaps because she had experienced serious illness. In her youth, she was a victim of rheumatic fever. An affliction that can cause death.

'You know, it is you that is keeping our spirits up.'

Though he never showed it around me, my father was very demoralised by the injury. It hit him hard that his eldest son, a former student international athlete had been reduced to living with paralysis. He saw the injury as akin to a life sentence.

'It's been a nightmare son but your approach is helping us a lot.'

My brother, on the other hand is perfectly healthy and still retains the invincibility of youth although he has passed 30.

'Well, I want to explain to all of you my approach in more detail.'

'State of mind, very important and I can appreciate it better than most.'

'First and foremost I will never accept the permanence of my paralysis. As long as my paralysis is present it is a fact of life yet I will continue to defy this lack of mobility. Since I now find myself in a situation where a definitive prognosis is unknown then defiance of prospective permanent disability seems natural.'

'Better than most judgments I've heard, possibly because you know the subject matter so well. You're talking about your own fighting spirit that will see you through the battle. A spirit laced with a strong dose of reasoning.'

'This defiance of mine has already got me noticed.'

'Oh, been a bold boy.'

'Not really bold dad but definitely defiant. One of the most experienced nurses was turning me in the bed this afternoon but as she turned me she brushed up against my scar and it hurt like hell. So I shouted at her. Then she gets indignant and says there is no way I could feel anything that low down my spine, of course, that made me shout even louder. How dare she assume where along my back I had sensation and where I did not.'

I believed and continue to believe that my recovery should not be shackled by any expectation with the exception of one, that is, a dogged determination to progress.

Five

Infection And Reflection

I WAS brought to the National Rehabilitation Hospital in Dun Laoghaire by ambulance on 25 February almost one month after the rugby match. One of the most striking aspects of 'Rehab' is its status as a hospital, in that the doctors tend to be led by the physiotherapists and not the other way around. The exception to this emphasis occurs when the patient is sick, that is to say when the patient is incapable of 'physio'.

Unfortunately the start of my physiotherapy was delayed by illness or more specifically by a pressure sore. It meant a three week stay in bed or as long as it took for the sore to clear. This waiting period before 'physio' was difficult because it meant a delay in any progression that might occur. It was during this initial period in bed that I began to recognise the differences between 'rehab' and the more acute hospital care of the National Spinal Unit. For instance, the clearest change in priority was the 'rehab' emphasis on functional independence.

When this concept was first explained to me I was truly disappointed because that was when I realised that the outcomes sought by the rehab practitioners were at odds with my own.

A difference of opinion was clearly evident between myself and the rehab staff.

I was told by the surgeons who performed the operation on my spinal cord that it was not severed therefore I was an incomplete spinal patient with expectations a good deal higher than my rehabilitation consultant.

I believed and continue to believe that my recovery should not be shackled by any expectation with the exception of one, that is, a dogged determination to progress from sitting to standing to walking, be that walking assisted or otherwise.

Conferences are meetings between the rehab team, the patient and any family members the patient requests to be present. My conference was held in an overly warm room without sufficient ventilation or windows. The consultant chaired the meeting and spoke first:

'Your stay in rehab will not be any longer than three months.'

'Why that particular time frame?'

'That is the duration associated with the schedule of physio and occupational therapy we have planned for you.'

'What do you expect me to be able to do when I leave?'

'Your level of functional independence will be such that you will be able to take care of your own bowel and bladder without assistance. You will have full control over your own wheelchair and be able to transfer in and out of it by yourself.'

'It is obvious you do not see walking in my immediate future. What about a full restoration of bowel and bladder?'

At this point the ward sister was about to say something encouraging but she was interrupted, almost before she began, by the consultant.

'Don't bother sister, the likelihood is that normal functioning will not return.'

'On the first occasion we spoke you stated that you could not definitively rule out the possibility of future improvement because of the nature of the injury. Is that still your view?'

'Yes.'

'Yet you could not be more definitive with regard to my stay in rehab.'

'Well I'm basing my opinion on experience.'

'I understand that but I want you to know, and everyone else in this room to know, you will not decide the outcome of this disability of mine. I will.'

A pause. Then the registrar of the consultant spoke:

'Your reaction of denial is to be expected, as a result, we have assigned a psychologist to your case should you wish to talk with her.'

My mother spoke next.

'Ciarán is a qualified behavioural scientist and has already formulated a psychological platform from which he will proceed.'

'That is all very well but it is our view that your disability is not by its nature passing. For our intents and purposes it is permanent.'

'If that is so then how come people have recovered and recovered completely?' asked my dad.

'Each injury varies in severity. In your son's case the damage could not be more severe.' replied the consultant.

'My surgeon has stated on more than one occasion: my spinal cord is not severed or transected. Therefore I am an incomplete spinal patient who sees his disability as one day ending.'

'I do not see your injury as incomplete,' he said.

'I will tell you what I mean by a temporary as opposed to a permanent disability. It is an affliction that disappears after a period of time. I do not know how long I will be afflicted but my gut tells me to be prepared not only for years but decades. At the same time always look forward to the day when you do walk again.'

The 'three month' stay in rehab proved to be inaccurate but primarily due to complications beyond anyone's control. I developed a bed sore. While the sore kept me in bed for three weeks, I was barely up when a clot was discovered at the back of my left knee. This was another reason why my stay in rehab proved to be longer than initially thought. The clot occurred almost one month after my arrival in rehab and meant a two-week stay in bed with a six month course of medication.

In bed, I read a number of books. One of these was given to me by my future sister-in-law, a book written by Steven Pressfield. My brother had been living and working in Milan since the previous September. While there he met and fell in love with a native

Milanese and they set August as the month they would marry. He proposed soon after my rugby match, so 2002 would at least have one bright moment to counter that dark one.

The message of Pressfield's book, 'Gates of Fire' came in the form of a question; 'What is the opposite of fear?' The answer given was love. This book was important because it encouraged me through my faith to challenge my fear of paralysis. As the two-week period of mandatory bed rest for the clot came to a close, I got a temperature. At this point I had hoped that the blood thinning medication I was receiving would be changed to another type of a lesser potency. I was being medicated with a substance that was also utilised to eradicate rats.

In short, it was believed that a recognised poison would eradicate my clot however by attempting to resolve one problem it created another. One that only showed itself about a month to six weeks after the start of going on the medication. However, well before this forthcoming complication my body temperature was up and initially the doctors thought it was a urinary tract infection so they treated it accordingly with an antibiotic. The temperature went away and the infection seemed to wane – however it was only a short respite.

At this time, the beginning of April, my cast was to be removed and replaced by an anterior shell. This shell supports the front of the trunk while the back has to work without the extra support of a cast or shell. It was the first time in six weeks that my trunk was exposed to the air. Something that struck me straight away was the musky smell of stale sweat. Once the cast was cut off completely with a pair of sheers there was a moment when I felt lighter, as if a great weight had been removed, even though the cast did not weigh very much.

The last time I had seen my chest was in the dressing room before the game. At that time, I was a healthy person with my physicality completely in tact but only six weeks on my body was broken. It struck me as a great pity that being free of the cast didn't mean I had shaken free of the disability. It was the first time in my life that I remained unhealthy after medical treatment had been given.

'They have done all they can do and you still can't move', said Fear.

'I have a full course of physiotherapy ahead of me', replied Faith.

'You heard what that consultant said moving in and out of a wheelchair that is one of the primary objectives of your planned physiotherapy. It sounded like the central tenet of their functional independence. This takes me back to the one question that just will not go away: how independent will you be?'

'The level of my independence will be greatly determined by the strides I make in physio.'

'Strides, very unfortunate choice of words.'

While getting the cast removed, certainly indicated progression, regression was never too far away.

The first regression was the return of another bed sore located as before around the sacrum. Sores are caused by infection, paralysis suppresses the immune system leaving the paraplegic open to infection. The other backward step proved to be a more serious complication and one I will return to in time. The second bed sore meant my stay, away from physio, continued but it did allow me plenty of time to think.

One of my more reassuring thoughts was the fact that while I was losing physio there was a second process underway – one that needed rest to gain fruition, it being the slow process of nerve regeneration. Doctors differ on this issue of nerve regeneration, specifically spinal nerve regeneration.

There are two trains of thought; firstly the view that there exists after a spinal trauma dead nerves and deadened nerves. The dead nerves are not capable of returning to their previous state of health but by way of contrast the deadened nerves are not only capable of returning to the their previous glory but have the capacity to increase their workload. That is to say these latter nerves fulfil their tasks as before and fulfil some of the tasks previously carried out by their dead colleagues.

Consequently, once sensation and movement is reactivated both are initially coarse and lacking refinement, but over time restoration of fine motor control returns. The second train of thought is less encouraging as it maintains that spinal nerves once damaged do not have the capacity to take on any extra workload. Thus sensation and movement once gone is lost forever.

The medical debate over spinal nerve rejuvenation is weighed down with the unknown. However, I sought mental refuge in the belief that spinal nerve rejuvenation was occurring within me. Thoughts, just continued to flow in and out of my mind. One such thought reoccurred regularly – why did the president of the club appear to agree with my assessment of the incident one day and change his mind a few days later.

Whatever the reason for his change of viewpoint he did not favour the idea of bringing a claim of negligence. He felt that should no case be brought, a quicker insurance payout by the rugby union would be more likely. I told him that my solicitor was assessing the situation and would help me make an informed decision. Another consideration that the president would be obliged to consider would be the possibility of me making an insurance claim against the club itself.

If this occurred then the cost of insuring playing members of the club would sky-rocket to the extent that it would become prohibitive to insure players. Given such a context it would be unlikely the club could attract anyone to play in the aftermath of my injury since the cost of insurance would ultimately be passed on to the players by way of their subscriptions. Whether such scenarios were influential or not, the fact remains the club since day one, has been highly supportive and not just in any abstract way but in very substantial ways.

For example, the club provided a laptop computer which in turn allowed me to watch the latest DVDs. Each Saturday or Sunday with my girlfriend we enjoyed a DVD together. She was a woman I admired, after all, it's not every woman who would want a dalliance with a man she meets in the intensive spinal care unit of a major hospital. A man faced with the medical view that he would not walk again. What were the prospects for this couple with the primary issue of health a constant concern.

In addition, there were the associated and magnified concerns of accessibility, transportation, accommodation and basic ablutions. None of these somewhat daunting prospects seemed to bother her. However she was intent on going abroad to teach for a contracted period of a year, which was to be followed by a six-month holiday period.

*I was approaching my
36th birthday and of my
36 years on this planet, only
one was in the chair, the other
35 years were not and I knew
where my preference lay.*

Six

A Fellow Patient

WHILE in hospital I met several patients, visitors and hospital staff but there was one person, however, who I tended to gravitate towards quite naturally and quite easily.

One day I introduced myself by telling her my name. I told her about my ill-fated return to rugby and she told me why she was in hospital and how it was not the first time she had been to rehab. At the age of four she had been knocked down. The damage to her spine was such that it would prove impossible for her to walk so she had been confined to a wheelchair ever since.

On this occasion, she was in hospital to remedy an ulcer that had developed from deep within her and had only recently manifested itself by breaking her skin. It was a condition that would not heal itself and required plastic surgery. After talking for a while it became clear that our experiences of being in wheelchairs clearly differed from each other. I was approaching my 36th birthday and of my 36 years on this planet, only one was in the chair, the other 35 years were not and I knew where my preference lay.

My attractive new friend with clearly defined features had an entirely different experience. Of her 28 years only four were not in a chair so she had a long time to adjust to the less than spectacular prospect of wheeling as opposed to walking through life. We discussed many things, a supportive family was one topic to which we returned more than once. Just looking around the ward and seeing how other patients had to manage with minimal support from family reminded us both how crucial family backing was in testing times.

As the days passed and we spoke to each other more often I found that I was becoming more attracted to this strikingly bright incisive woman.

While this attraction grew, my testing times continued for it was not until the end of April, that I had my first shower in about a month. Prior to that showering proved impossible because of the position of the sore. It was on the sacrum an area that would be pressurised while taking a shower lying down on a shower trolley however progress could be reported in other areas; I was about to start self-catheterisation and was administering suppositories to myself.

In other words, the finer details of functional independence were becoming a reality.

Furthermore, it was about this time too that the anterior shell was due to be removed allowing my trunk to be unfettered for the first time in three months. This, in turn, would allow me to lie on my front, something that was very important, because it would relieve pressure and stiffness around the hips and pelvis by giving them a much needed rest.

Another facet of functional independence was the use of a shower chair. This chair is designed to allow the person in the seating position to shower himself without any assistance. Showering that way was another facet of functional independence. Progression was occurring on another front.

Before going to rehab I had never heard of occupational therapy. It is a very necessary part of rehabilitation given its concentration on adaptation of the house, adaptation of the work environment and adaptation of transportation, all prerequisites of functional independence.

At this time, car transfers were practised from my wheelchair to the mock-up car and then transferring back again. When transferring from the chair the person is in a position to choose whether or not to put his legs into the car first or the upper half of his body. My preference was for the legs first and the rest thereafter. Occupational therapy in the mornings was followed by lunch that in turn was followed by the 'tilt table' at physiotherapy in the afternoons.

The 'tilt table' is a hard flat mechanised table capable of bringing the patient from the horizontal position to the vertical position with the aid of straps and the press of a button. It is a precursor to other devices designed to assist the patient to stand.

It was the first week in May and I was having half an hour of occupational therapy in the morning and an hour of physiotherapy in the afternoons.

Seven

Humour, Transportation And Wedding Preparation

O NE morning, the ward sister approached me. She was a woman not to be taken lightly. She was someone who exuded a natural authority. An individual who commanded respect while always maintaining an air of business-like activity. Underneath it all though was a sense of humour.

'You know you wink at me a lot,' she said

'I wasn't aware I winked at you,' I replied.

'But you do, not with your eyes but with your backside,' she said matter-of-factly.

'Really, I was completely unaware I had such an active rear end.'

'You do, in fact your anus winks at me and most others you pass by.'

'So it's not picky, any bum will do.'

That last comment did bring the suggestion of a smile to this senior nurse.

'You have what is called an 'anal wink', it implies that sacral nerves are still working. It's actually a good sign.'

'That's a relief for one fleeting second I thought I had a defective backside.'

'Call over that nurse over there and ask her have you been winking at her lately because you been constantly winking at me.'

'So you're wondering if it's becoming a habit.'

I called the nurse over and put the question to her as sincerely as I could. There was a pause and her expression was such that she may have thought I was losing it. It was at this juncture that the ward sister started to laugh, and said:

'Remember that research paper we were discussing yesterday

about involuntary control of the sacral nerves?'

With that question the expression on the nurse's face went quickly from bewilderment to embarrassment. The moral of the story maybe, not to show someone your backside because you can never be sure, what you'll get in return.

A necessary but unfortunate aspect of paralysis is bowel care. Aside from the heightened sense of awareness regarding my bodily functions, I was building up a schedule again, it was the first week in May and I was having half an hour of occupational therapy in the morning and an hour of physiotherapy in the afternoons.

As a wheelchair-bound person, I am entitled to exemptions from vehicle registration tax, value added tax and excise duty. In addition I was entitled to a once-off back to work grant. In early May I took advantage of these benefits and bought a top of the range specially adapted diesel automatic. Together, with the car salesman, I wheeled myself out to inspect the car which had been parked in a direct line to the hospital entrance. It was a china blue Peugeot 406.

'... has it been adapted? Can I sit in?'

'It has and you can.'

'How is it altered exactly?'

'Firstly, it's an automatic, so you won't have to worry about changing gears. Secondly, there is a hand-controlled lever to the right of the steering wheel which is directly connected to both the accelerator and brake. By pulling the lever up you go forward and by pressing the lever down you stop.'

'Is there central locking with an internal alarm?'

'Yes.'

And with that he gave me the keys. I opened the doors and transferred from my chair to the driving seat something which I had practised in occupational therapy, though not too often. The feeling of sitting behind the wheel has never felt so good. I was finally in a position to carry out an activity that hardly differed at all from before the injury.

The first drive in the car took place on the same day as a general election. It was a very wet day but after having voted I was driven down to my old school and practised driving in an empty car park. The feeling I got from an activity that previously had been taken for granted was more than elation. It was a fresh sense of renewal, spurred on by an independence only a moving vehicle can convey. I was driven back to rehab but by the next weekend I drove back to rehab from a home visit myself.

My parents, returned from their first trip to Italy a few days after the car was delivered to me out in rehab. They found out that there are a number of differences between an Italian and an Irish wedding, firstly, there is no such thing as one best man at this Italian-Irish wedding. In fact there would be three; myself, my brother and the brother of the wife-to-be.

Usually, in northern Italy, the wedding ceremony in the morning is followed by an afternoon dinner and guests would return home in the early evenings. However the Irish influence would be brought to bear here as well. When it comes to dressing for the occasion the Italians tend not to dress as formally as we Irish like to.

As I lay on my side, I noticed I could move my knee up towards my chest and then with some effort I could push it back down again.

Eight

New Movement – And Another Infection

D URING the last week in May I started the process of self-intermittent catheterisation, yet another example of functional independence. Before starting this process, I had a leg bag attached during the day and bed bag attached at night. These bags essentially equated to permanent catheterisation and were necessary to combat incontinence of the bladder. The problem with having a 'foreign body' like a catheter in place within the body is its potential as a source of infection, and unfortunately, I was having urinary tract infections regularly. By 'regularly' I mean about one a month.

This initial phase of learning about the catheter proved to be painful but that in itself was not such a bad experience. Simply put, pain is a form of sensation and to feel pain the conveyors of pain, the nerves, must be intact. I felt pain, therefore the sacral nerves associated with the bladder were at least partially intact. At this time I did something that was completely unexpected and was a very pleasant surprise.

As I lay on my side, I noticed I could move my knee up towards my chest and then with some effort I could push it back down again. I turned over onto my other side and attempted to do the same with the other knee and found that I could move in the same way on both sides. I decided the first person I would show this movement to would be my physiotherapist.

'I have some good news, not news I want to tell, more like news that needs to be shown.'

My physiotherapist, at that time, was young, enthusiastic and at all times constructive.

'OK, let's have it.'

I turned onto my side and brought my knee towards my chest then repeated the process on the other side. I could see my physiotherapist was delighted for me but he did not say anything immediately. Instead he brought the senior physio over to ask her for an opinion.

'Ok, Ciarán show us the movement you've got.'

When the senior physio saw the movement she asked me:

'Could you repeat that movement three times?'

I did.

'That movement implies you have voluntary control over movement emanating from the nerves associated with the L1 to L3 vertebrae.'

'That means, nerve impulses are getting through the trauma and initiating movement below the level of the lesion.'

'Yes.'

'It also means that my diagnosis of being T12 complete is wrong. I must be incomplete.'

'It appears that way but physios do not decide diagnoses only doctors.'

Given this restored movement the physiotherapists now considered me to be 'incomplete,' giving at least a modicum of hope that I would walk again. The doctors, however, even when shown my restored new movement did not change their diagnosis for some time. Yet this was one moment when triumph mixed with vindication. It was the time when my thoughts, feelings and knowledge about my diagnosis proved to be accurate.

About a week after I discovered the restored movement, I had my first reflexology session and for the first time I felt some sensation around the balls of my feet. The hospital did not provide reflexology, instead a friend of the family offered her services on the basis that it was the best thing she could do for me. She has trained in a number of alternative treatments but was of the view that reflexology was my best option.

Not only did I feel some sensation around the balls of my feet but when I placed my feet on the ground I could feel some weight go through them. While this was good news it was not the news I really wanted because the slight sensation only occurred randomly; it was not ever present. In addition to the sensation, reflexology reduced swelling around my ankles and induced relaxation throughout my body.

Towards the end of May some four months after the rugby match I was told that I had an arthritic infection in my left hip. The infection was away from the hip joint, something that was important especially given the fact that any restored movement I did have was all emanating from my hips. In short an assault on my hips was a direct assault on my restored movement.

The symptoms of the infection were varied; my hips were very painful especially when touched and when I lay on them, a mottled purple patch appeared just below my left hip running down the outside of my thigh and my temperature was difficult to control.

Hetrotopic ossification was diagnosed. This is unwanted bone spurs growing into both soft tissue and bone; it is also referred to as calcification. It is not uncommon in a person suffering from paralysis however the rapid manifestation combined with the very high temperatures that were apparent in my case was unusual. Various antibiotics were used to kill the infection yet none seemed to prevail.

One day a visiting orthopaedic consultant came to my bedside and asked the pertinent question that ultimately resolved the issue. He asked was I being prescribed any anti-coagulants. I told him I was. His response was that such medication should stop because it was the root cause of the calcification and infection. He then outlined how this process took place.

As I worked hard at the physiotherapy and being on the blood-thinning medication to counteract the clot, that first showed itself in March, internal bleeding occurred resulting in a drop in the iron content of my blood and an abnormal stimulation of bone growth, that in turn caused infection. Prior to this diagnosis, I was sent for various scans to rule out more serious scenarios, on one such occasion I was sent back to the Mater where I met the registrar of the surgeon who worked on me.

'Hi, how are you?'

'Not bad, over-worked under-appreciated which is pretty much normal.'

'Do you have a few minutes?'

'Sure. Do you want to show me something?'

'I certainly do.'

Then I turned on my side and brought my knee up to my chest repeating the same movement on the other side.

'That is pre-ambulatory movement, although I am not an expert in physiotherapy, it's a good advance. Well done; you must be doing your physio regularly.'

'Well, I am.'

'It shows. Now with regard to the unwanted bone growth, it is too close to the emergency surgery of January last to have another operation to remove the bone spurs.'

'Why is that?'

'Your body or more specifically your bones need up to two years if not longer to fully recuperate after your operation. If we operated too quickly more virulent bone spurs could take hold. So surgery at this time would be inadvisable.'

'What are the alternatives?'

'Anti-inflammatories.'

'I'm not keen because of what they can do to the lining of the stomach.'

'Some are certainly harder on the stomach than others.'

'I am in pain so it looks like I have little choice.'

'Just try to limit the time you take them.'

Throughout this period I remained unsettled, for I knew the unwanted calcium was attacking the most influential joints for walking, my hips.

'Just when you thought progress was underway, what happens? One sad story after another,' said Fear.

'You did hear what that registrar said about my movement: pre-ambulatory was the word he used. That is, movement leading up to or prior to walking', replied Faith.

'Of course, as he said he's no expert.'

'No, but at the same time he just happened to be in that operating theatre working on me. So I think he does have some medical expertise.'

'Without the surgery the bone spurs could inhibit your physiotherapy. Proper stretching and movement around the hips will become increasingly difficult.'

'Only if I ignore the advice given to me.'

Once in the car my father gave me directions. It was obvious we were not driving home; instead we were travelling directly into town.

Nine

Movement And Other Forms Of Rehab

THE various movements I had to date continued to point to the fact that mine was an incomplete spinal cord injury though as mentioned before it took the doctors a long time to accept this view.

Their position continued to reflect the devastating impact of the burst fracture and their experience of patients with similar fractures whom they had treated. One day my father arrived early in the morning. I thought it was unusual since he would normally come in the evenings. He must have taken the day off which is also very much out of the ordinary.

'Let's go.'

'Let's go where?'

'To the car. It's time you took it for a proper spin.'

'Ok, but does anyone here know about this mysterious trip.'

'Well they know you're going for a drive but they do not know where.'

'And neither do I.'

'Come on, you'll soon find out.'

Once in the car my father gave me directions. It was obvious we were not driving home; instead we were travelling directly into town.

'I'm going to work.'

'Yes, I've told your colleagues to expect a surprise. I think they're expecting chocolate to have at their coffee break.'

'I hope you have chocolate somewhere close then.'

'I do, but this is more than just an excuse for an extended coffee break.'

'It's all about access.'

'Well, it's mostly about access but it's also a timely reminder to your employers that you intend to return to work as soon as you're ready for it.'

As Business Manager, I have control over the company's finances as well as responsibility for the distribution and marketing of publications. The building where I work has a basement car park from which I can take a lift to the third floor of the building. It's there that my office is located with door locks and handles all within reach. The toilet facilities, however, were not as they should be, as there was no wheelchair toilet available in the building. The nearest was in the next building over and across the adjacent car park.

'How are you? It's good to see you? Are you finished with rehab? Are you going back? What's happening?'

'I'm fine, not finished with rehab and should be on the way back this afternoon.'

'So you're just here to spy on us. To see if we're behaving ourselves.'

'That's it I could only leave you reprobates on your own for so long before remedial action would be essential. No, I'm just looking at the building from an accessibility perspective.'

'And...'

'Well, it's OK except for the toilets.'

'We know about that and we've been on to building services. They say that they recognise the need and a purpose built toilet should be in place within the next year.'

'Surprisingly fast considering their less than speedy approach to life.'

'How's the rehab going?'

'I'm working what works and trying to work what doesn't.'

'Well you definitely look better than the time we went to the hospital.'

'I agree all those tubes sticking out of me just wasn't my look.

It's fine, I'm allowed make jokes like that. Seriously though, I'm stronger and I do have more sensation but it is a slow uphill battle.'

'When can you start work again?'

'Well there's no talk about when but the powers that be do believe I should be able to work again. For me that's what is important.'

After about two hours or so I drove back to rehab from town. The pleasure I got driving in town, was liberating. I was doing something anew something that had been second nature and then taken away from me. The little trip in town was essentially unsanctioned and soon after my return to the hospital I got a urinary tract infection so perhaps, I should have delayed my drive. Even though my temperature started to rise I did not regret either the timing or the carrying out of my visit to the world of work. For me it was a further exercise in rehabilitation as would be the sanctioned visit to the 'Villa Maria' on the grounds of the hospital itself.

The 'Villa Maria' is a specially designed house for wheelchair-bound people. It is a single-floor dwelling with four bedrooms, kitchen, dining/sitting room and hall. All the household appliances are within reach of the seated person. Two of the bedrooms have bathrooms ensuite, each with properly dimensioned toilet bowls and wheel-in showers. I shared my stay with my family. The stay lasted for two days at the end of which I returned to the ward. Unfortunately during that weekend at the villa I had an infection that spread from the urethra to a testicle. As a result the testicle swelled up to enormous proportions not something that lifted my spirits; however, life was not all bad news.

With just a month to go to the wedding, I decided to set myself the target of standing in front of my family, for the first time since January. It was going to require practice and hard work but that was something I was looking forward to. Within a week after the fitting of splints, I stood in the gym between the parallel bars. I also celebrated my 36th birthday. Standing between the bars was not the safest option for me as their low height forced me to compromise my vertical balance. This led to a pitching forward of my trunk and excessive uneven weight on my hips.

To overcome this difficulty, my physiotherapist and myself decided to stand with the splints on in the standing frame. This allowed me to straighten up and get more benefit from the exercise, though being in the standing frame meant further straps were attached to support my backside.

This assistance was reduced over time forcing the hips to independently carry more and more body weight. The older standing frames are wooden frames designed like a 'baby bouncer,' without any attachment to the ceiling and with long poles that act as arm rests.

To progress from the standing frame to the correct height parallel bars, standing with splints in the frame for 20 minutes is advisable. Of course when it came to the wedding neither standing frame nor bars would be available. Necessity would have to be the mother of invention.

It was the first time I ever spent my birthday in hospital. As a family usually we celebrated by eating out. We did this the weekend before the birthday. On the day, I got a signed card from the staff on the ward and another from the admissions office. I also had a visit that day from my girlfriend.

'Hi, birthday boy I've got a present for you.'

'Do you think I deserve a present – I mean have I been a good boy?'

'Not bad, could show improvement though.'

'Oh God, sounds like a school report, satisfactory but...'

'Anyway lean forward, close your eyes and only open them when I say.'

I did as I was told and when I looked at what had been put around my neck, I said: 'That was unnecessary.'

'Maybe but I wanted you to have it all the same. It is a gold cross given to me by my grandfather for my first holy communion.'

That was the first time it hit me. While I was attracted to this woman, I was not in love with her and what spelt it out was this very personal and sentimental gift. I did not deserve this symbol of sacrifice. It was a situation where my heart and mind were consumed with a single focus of attention, my recovery.

I was not in a position to share myself in a deeply committed way. Any and all commitment I could muster was reflected inwards not outwards. We never discussed this self-centred emphasis of mine. To be honest, I suspect that the woman in question knew that I was emotionally unavailable.

A strong personal desire burns within though; it was the need to do all that I could to regain full health.

Ten

Mirrors, Hair Cuts, Sport And Frustration

LYING in bed for as long as I did had a number of psychological effects on me. Some were more obvious than others; the need for patience yet wanting total recovery as soon as possible and determination to do all that I could to bring about progress in my condition.

These two psychological aspects of my make-up were at times glaringly apparent and have remained so, however more subtle psychological aspects concerned use of mirrors, a return to any form of competitive sport and getting a haircut. None of these three activities held any appeal, whatsoever. Given the need to monitor 'would be sores', the use of a mirror was the first of these three activities that I struggled to carry out. The ward sister approached me more than once regarding the purchase of a mirror.

'It's important you monitor your skin.'

'As long as I'm in this bed, I don't feel like monitoring anything.'

She then spoke to the nearest nurse.

'Would you go to the shop and find out the price of a mirror.'

'Yes, sister.'

The ward sister waited for the nurse to return and in the meantime asked about my family and in particular how the wedding preparations were going. The nurse came back within a few minutes.

'The price is 80 cents, sister.'

'That is a very good price. Here's the money for one.'

The conversation turned to the weather and specifically whether or not we would we have anything resembling a summer.

We didn't as it turned out. The nurse was back almost as quickly as the last time. Only this time he was holding a newspaper.

'The Mirror costs only eighty cents. Then again tabloids are better priced than the broadsheets.'

I think it would be fair to say that the sister found it difficult to see the humour. The nurse knew about my disdain for mirrors but I think it was a genuine mistake rather than a deliberate action on his part.

Nevertheless, I remained in no hurry to purchase a mirror. Some of my reluctance was undoubtedly due to me being stuck in a hospital bed taking what I thought was a long time to recover and as long as I was 'stuck' I felt no desire to see myself, from any angle at all.

A strong personal desire burns within though; it is the need to do all that I could to regain full health. Whether that means buying a mirror or being woken at two in the morning to empty my bladder, then that is what I would do.

Eventually, the mirror was bought, the skin was monitored and I minded less and less looking at himself stuck in bed. The lack of a haircut was never as much a contentious issue as the acquisition of a mirror, though staff and visitors alike were not slow to remind me of how I needed to have my hair cut.

Before hospitalisation I would have a cut about once every three months. It was about a month to go before the August wedding and I had my last cut the previous December. So I promised my brother I would get it cut for his wedding.

As August approached, I was allowed to go home at weekends. I would be driven from the hospital on Saturday mornings and driven back Sunday evenings. Being at home, though wonderful, only heightened the constraints of being in the wheelchair. There were no ramps around the house and I could not get to a toilet or my own bed. Under these conditions 'functional independence' is farcical. It was during one of these trips that I diverted to my local barber.

'You'll have to pull me backwards up the step so I can get into the barber's.'

'That's fine, but it's a pity there's no ramp or better still a flat entrance.'

So my father pulled me into the shop. The barber looked at me with a shocked expression.

'I didn't know it was you.'

'What do you mean?'

'You were the one that was injured playing rugby. I heard someone from CYM was injured. I just didn't know it was you. Christ, how are you?'

'Well still in rehab but let out for the day.'

'What about recovery?'

'The doctors are not exactly optimistic but at the same time they admit to a lack of knowledge when it comes to this type of injury.'

'Some people do recover.'

'Yes, but it depends entirely on the severity of the injury.'

'I take it yours was severe.'

'Unfortunately, yes.'

'Still, are you doing physio?'

'Everyday.'

Soon enough the conversation turned to football. The barber had begun to relax. His reactions were typical of the way people react to me in a wheelchair. Shock is a common reaction from people who have known me from before and who then meet me as I am now. People witness first hand the massive shift from foot mobility to chair mobility; then they start listening to me carrying on as if this change is almost a natural one. Not long after this point, a nervousness sets in because people start saying to themselves he can not be this calm about his circumstances. After a further period, people relax on the basis that maybe he has learned to live with it and if he is alright with the wheelchair, so should I.

Since 27 January 2002, I have not been involved in any

competitive sport and unlike mirrors or haircuts, this situation remained unchanged. For me sport has always been a great outlet for the release of tension from everyday life. However, when that outlet became a source of serious injury, then my attitude to participating in it changed, I no longer had any desire to compete.

As the wedding approached, so too did the six-month anniversary of the match. The medical people always made plain how they were essentially practising an area of medicine that little was known about. My phrase for this context was 'don't know medicine', yet they felt the six-month mark was a significant one.

Their view is that any improvements in movement and or sensation tend to primarily occur by six months, thereafter, if any improvements occur they tend to be either so incrementally small that they are insignificant or irrelevant to a full restoration of normality. For me the end of July 2002 was my supposed watershed and quite simply I felt frustrated because apart from patchy sensation in my left thigh and some signs of hip flexion, I was no nearer to standing and walking than I had been in January.

My frustration was due in no small part to my succession of infections, sores, a clot and a distinct lack of physiotherapy due to bed confinement. Whenever frustration set in, fear was never too far behind though despite this groundswell of angst, I retained what Koreans refer to as 'Han', that is, an enduring sense of hope at a time when it is irrational.

'Face it you're going nowhere', said Fear.

'I'm just progressing slowly', replied Faith.

'Really, what form does this slow progress take?'

'Wearing you down is the slow progress I'm referring to.'

'As long as the future remains unknown you will never wear be down.'

'Ah yes, ignorance, the driving force behind fear but you'll find my raison d'etre to be equally sustaining.'

'So what might that be?'

'Strength of character.'

'We'll see.'

'Yes, we will.'

In conjunction with the frustration and fear I felt a growing sense of futility. My response to it was to stand when in Italy for my brother's wedding. I told this to my physiotherapist and he was worried about the safety aspect of it. His suggestion was to have two high-backed chairs to my left and right and perhaps one in front so as I stood up from my wheelchair I could grip the chairs for the support I would need.

In addition, I was going to need a person in each chair to stabilise them when I was in the standing position. Before all that, I needed to practice my standing in the standing frame and I needed to go to Italy knowing I could stand, with less support than a standing frame could provide. Instead of such strong support I would have to make do with my bi-lateral splints which, while supportive, are not as strong as the frame.

Throughout this at times frustrating period, I still enjoyed getting into my car and driving. As I already mentioned one aspect of occupational therapy is to rehabilitate the patient back behind a steering wheel again. With this in mind I had a driving lesson specially organised by rehab. I explained to the driving instructor how I had been driving back to rehab each weekend and on one occasion had driven in town. We took the lesson in my car and by the end of the 40 minute drive, he admitted he learned more from me than I could have from him.

I was scheduled over the following fortnight to have two further lessons with him but they fell through because of an infection one week and my trip to Italy the next . I met up with the instructor after I returned and made my excuses for not taking the remaining lessons. He told me that the trip to Italy was definitely a more attractive excuse. I couldn't but agree.

My physio no longer saw me as 'complete' instead he maintained that I was 'incomplete'. It is the one and only instance that I have ever craved to be 'incomplete' at anything.

Eleven

Arthritis, A Chair,
A Claim And A Wedding

G IVEN the state of the arthritis or more accurately the calcification evident in my hips, it was decided that a review would take place at the end of August, the purpose of which would be to decide whether surgery would be beneficial at that time, or not. To avoid surgery no further unwanted bone growth or calcification could occur. Needless to say further surgery would only hinder any progression I might make so it was something that I did not desire.

The hope was that the medication I was taking would be sufficient to halt the deterioration in my hips or perhaps, reverse the progression of this aggressive condition. A reversal, brought about by the medication however was unlikely. While it can occur it only does so in very few instances so no disimprovement in the situation was likely to be the best I could hope for. With a full month to go before the decision to operate, I decided to keep such thoughts to the back of my mind.

In the meantime, I was given a new chair to try out. Each patient is encouraged to try a number of different choices until he or she decides on what is the most suitable. I had been sitting in a heavy one with a large turning circle. It was also non-folding making transportation of it limited to the boot of a car and, having said that, not every boot would be suitable. My preference had to be more suitable to my needs.

Above all else I wanted a light folding model that I could keep in the front passenger seat as I drove along. That way, I would not be dependent on others to put it in the boot once I had transferred into the driver's seat. The chair I selected had what I was looking for. It was light, folding and had a small turning circle. It would now allow me to drive without any assistance... a welcome return to normality.

Also at this time – the end of July 2002 – I was given an Asia test, often referred to as the gold standard of tests for paralysis.

'Hi Ciarán, I have all the bits and pieces necessary for this test. Are you OK to do this now, no physio or occupational therapy or anything like.'

'Now would be fine.'

'OK, I'll touch you with both the needle and the cotton wool intermittently. So just let me know if you can feel anything, where you're feeling it and what you're feeling.'

To begin the doctor placed the needle and or the cotton wool above the area of the injury. I had no difficulty determining one from the other. Then he proceeded to various areas of the body below the level of the injury.

'Do you feel anything here?'

He had placed a needle in contact with my skin about three-quarters way down my left thigh.

'Yes, but it is a distant feeling.'

He repeated the process on my right thigh but I felt nothing.

'Well you have improved slightly on the last test which is good news.'

'Yes, but what a long way to go.'

'All in good time. You must remember it is possible to regress with this test.'

'Really, I didn't know that.'

'Unfortunately that is the nature of paralysis.'

'You still diagnose me as having a complete injury.'

'Yes, but there'll be more tests and few things in medicine are guaranteed.'

My joy with the latest Asia test was somewhat limited given the difference of opinion between my doctors and physiotherapist. My physio no longer saw me as 'complete' instead he maintained that I was 'incomplete'. It is the one and only instance that I have ever craved to be incomplete at anything.

Another area that remained incomplete was the legal position surrounding the circumstances of my injury. Statements had been taken by my solicitor from players involved on the day and having sought feedback from a barrister, my solicitor maintained that an insurance claim had a better chance of succeeding than any possible civil suit. A claim could only be made after the end of January 2003. This news came with about a week to go to the wedding, as did my second conference. Normally, a second conference would have occurred within three months.

In my case there was no point given my succession of illnesses and infections. Just like the first conference, my entire medical care team were around the table along with myself and my parents.

'I'd like to begin by welcoming you all here today,' said the consultant.

'Thank you and let's hope I'm well enough to travel to Italy.'

The consultant turned to her registrar and asked about my latest infection.

'We intend to weigh Ciarán in order to determine the correct dosage of antibiotic to give him.'

'How long before the Italian trip?'

'Ten days.'

'That being so, give the antibiotics both orally and intravenously. By so doing we increase the likelihood of you travelling with your family for the wedding.'

I found the consultant's approach both constructive and encouraging.

'Have you arranged for occupational therapy to take a look at your house?'

'No, not yet.'

Alterations to the family home were very low on my 'to do' list. For me this was an area I did not want to address at all because it had a permanence associated with it that held no appeal whatsoever.

'Have you done anything regarding house alterations?'

'Yes, my occupational therapist has made some written suggestions and we have had a structural engineer take a look at them.'

'You need plans drawn up.'

'We'll have that done by the next meeting.'

It was the occupational therapist's turn to speak.

'Ciarán knows about the local authority grant for house alterations for the disabled and has told me he will pursue it.'

At that point my father interjected:

'The grant will be paid retrospectively which is understandable but the amount will only cover the cost of installing a lift. Ramps and other alterations will have to be met by ourselves, is that the case?'

'Yes it is. One positive is the short time your particular local authority takes in paying the grant.'

'Good but I take it there is no equivalent grant or subsidy to change the house back to its original state when no further need of these alterations arises.'

'No, there is just the once off payment and no more.'

Within hours of that second conference my faith in a future without paralysis was under fire.

'One thing is obvious, those doctors do not expect any change soon. It appears to me like they orient the patient towards the permanence of disability', said Fear.

'They are trying to control patients' levels of expectation', replied Faith.

'Really, by saying expect nothing because nothing is what you'll get.'

'By preparing for the worst but all the time hoping for improvement.'

'Sorry, maybe I missed something in that conference because I didn't hear one word about improvement. All I got was change the house or suffer the consequences.'

'Any changes that are made can be reversed.'

'Absolutely, but only if there is cause to do so.'

'You know, that comment proves to me I can always depend on your firm grasp of the obvious.'

Within a few days after that conference I stood between the parallel bars with just my splints to support me. In effect, this meant that standing at my brother's wedding, even for a very short time, was now a feasible option. I left the hospital on a Monday and took my first air trip as a wheelchair-bound person the next day. Over the weekend we prepared for the trip by removing from the hospital my clothes, medicines, medical supplies, books and everything else both necessary and unnecessary. My car could not stay parked in the hospital and had to be brought home for the duration of our stay in Italy.

The flight to Milan was at 7. 30am with the check-in time two hours earlier. I have always thought it wise to empty the bladder before travelling. Especially when getting up and going to the toilet during flight is not an option. Having checked in we made our way to the departure gate. Then about 10 minutes before anyone else got onto the plane, two men with green coats appeared and asked me my name.

I confirmed with them I was who they were expecting and with that we made our way out to the plane. Normally I would have been put onto a hydraulic vehicle. It also serves as a lift from which I could transfer into the plane. This vehicle/lift however was out of service. When we got to the foot of the steps the men asked me did I need help to move from my chair to a narrower chair. As it turned out I could manage.

Once sitting in this temporary form of transport I was strapped in and carried up the steps into the plane. In the plane, I was brought down the aisle to my seat and transferred with the help of the two men. Getting on the plane was different to getting off. Once we landed I was told I would have to wait until the plane was empty before it was my turn to set 'wheel' on terra firma, so first on but last off.

As with Dublin, the Milan hydraulic vehicle was out of service. Instead of two men with green coats, three men dressed in grey appeared with the now familiar narrow chair. When we reached the exit of the plane I could see my wheelchair placed besides the steps ready for me to transfer into it. After a shaky trip down the steps, with men who were clearly tiring in the sunshine, I sat there, quietly satisfied because I had achieved my first objective to be in Italy for my brother's wedding.

My second objective, was to show my family that they would not always see me sitting down rather than standing up and finally, I wanted to give the best man speech for my brother. My opportunity for standing came a few days after we arrived in Italy. It was a gathering of both families, as was the case every day, for an evening meal.

Before we sat down to eat, I stood up to instil hope within the people that meant most to me knowing that despair was beginning to take a grip. I had taken my leg splints to Italy so I put them on, transferred from the bed to the chair, wheeled into position between two chairs with a man sitting in each. I also had someone stand behind my wheelchair, to hold it as I grabbed hold of the two high-backed chairs in front of me, to my left and right.

It played out as planned with my physio back in rehab. Having grabbed both chairs I levered my way up into a standing position and managed to stand unaided by other people for about 15 seconds before I flopped back down into my wheelchair. It was the first time my family had seen me stand since January. Relief, elation and joy swept through the group and lightened the mood all round.

The day of the wedding came with over 60 Italians and about 20 Irish guests present. It was a morning wedding with an afternoon running into the evening reception. It was a superb day, by far the best day of 2002.

My brother was marrying a gentle, intelligent and spirited woman. A woman who shares both a similar outlook and set of religious beliefs as my brother. From the time I first saw them together in early January, I had a very strong feeling that they were well matched. Not only was I impressed by this woman, I was also very impressed with her family. Her father was a retired banker, her brother a working banker held in high esteem by his colleagues and her mother a person of the highest human qualities. This was the new familial background to which I gave my best man speech.

I began my speech by saying how unsurprised I was to learn that my brother had proposed marriage and that this proposal was accepted post haste. I felt they were well matched and I had no difficulty in repeating my view to anyone who cared to listen and several who cared not to.

My speech concentrated on the three traditional vows of marriage and how they had already tested the happy couple. A married man and a woman stay together through sickness and in health. While neither of them suffered any illness in the lead-up to marriage they did suffer indirectly. In addition, to the worry of my condition my brother's father-in-law had been ill. Not only was it serious but at one point looked like being life-threatening.

The bond of marriage is subject to financial stress – for richer or poorer. At the time of his wedding my brother had yet to find a job so naturally I made an impassioned plea to the wedding party, when I asked, if there was anyone in the audience in a position to provide him with work, could they please do so.

The third and perhaps the most testing vow of marriage is time – until death do us part. In the lead-up to the wedding, my brother was working for the summer in Ireland and during that time he was never too far away from a telephone so much so that when any telephone rang, he would answer it immediately and be delighted or let down, depending on whether it was his 'intended' at the other end of the line or not. I ended my speech by toasting the balance that exists between the happy couple and wished them a serene future together.

My first assisted walk lasted until I reached the other end of the gym – by which time I was finding it hard to stay vertical.

Twelve
Walking, Hydrotherapy And Leg Braces

SOON after my return from Italy I was about my daily routine of rehab. Only one day was not quite so usual.

'How was the trip?' asked my physio.

'Great, a little tiring but satisfying.'

'Did you stand?'

'I did, not for long, but certainly without anyone holding me up.'

'Good, I have a surprise.'

He went off to the other side of the gym and returned with a standing and walking support device. When I saw it I thought more practice standing. So I then put on my leg splints for secure support as I stood up.

'More standing.'

'Yes, but you're going to take a few steps today.'

How would it go? Would I be able to move anything? Was it too soon to try? I was determined, this was the first opportunity I had to walk and I was about to give it my very best. Sitting on the edge of the plinth with my legs straight out in front of me I grabbed hold of the device and hauled myself up into a standing position.

I took a few deep breaths and started to move my left leg from the hip. It was stiff and tight but I managed to slowly drag the leg through by about six inches before I stopped and gathered myself to repeat the process with the right leg. I had a person on my left and my right with my physio in front pulling the device forward as I tried to move. The pair at my sides had each foot wrapped in a sling which they moved as I tried to move one leg at a time.

My first assisted walk lasted until I reached the other end of the gym. By which time I was finding it hard to stay vertical. I was very tired but very satisfied I'd done it – a walk – the first in seven months.

The first inkling I had that assisted walking would be a possibility occurred a few days before my first steps. I noticed that I could maintain my balance while on all fours. Soon after this discovery, I tried to propel myself forwards and backwards by crawling – and I managed to do so. This confirmed two things: that there was indeed movement around my hips and that this movement was getting stronger.

The senior physio in the gym, however, did have a worry. She was concerned about my hips and how tight they were, it seemed to her, that they were in flexion quite a lot. By this she meant I seemed to be bent forward around the hips a good deal of the time, a position that does not lend itself to fluent walking. Having said that, however, my crawling was truly independent movement. There were no splints to assist and no people around to hold me in position. I could also engage in pelvic tilting – that is, being on all fours and bending the back in a concave and convex movement, thus strengthening the base of the back.

About a week after my first walk I had my first hydrotherapy session. As the name suggests this is physical therapy in water. What is not conveyed in the name is the fact that the water is heated to the same temperature as the body. After having changed, patients transfer onto a specially designed chair that can be attached to a hoist device and from there are lowered into the pool. Once in the water any movement a patient has appears to be exaggerated due to the buoyancy of the fluid environment. For example, in the water I was able to do sit-ups whereas on land this was not at all possible.

I had been scheduled to have a second hydro session that week but that was cancelled. Instead, I was pencilled in to visit a shop in town that sells household devices for people with disabilities, such as shower units, lifts (stair lifts and through the floor lifts). An occupational therapist had come out to our house the previous week and approved the plans for adapting the house submitted to her by the structural engineer.

The engineer, was a member of the Ciarán McCarthy fundraising committee, set up by my rugby club. Initially, I was reluctant to visit such a shop but over time I realised that the hospital were willing to hold on to me for a limited time only and I did not want to be sent back home to a house not adapted to receive me.

Going to the shop was another first, in that it was the first occasion that I drove in town on my own in the car. My parents together with the structural engineer went in another car. I followed them simply because they knew where they were going. The occupational therapist joined us later. After a while we all sat down and snacked at the on-site café.

'I broadly approved of the plans, you submitted but there are just a few details I'd like to mention.'

'Please, let's get them sorted out now, so we can save time later on.'

'I noticed you're planning to put the vanity unit in the bathroom next to the shower.'

'Only if there's enough room, otherwise I'll put it into the bedroom coming out from the back wall.'

'Good, because I think the more room in the bathroom the better. Your choice of floor covering for the bathroom is very durable with a non-slip surface. That is important with the shower chair spreading excess water all over it.'

'The wheel-in shower unit, happens to fit the dimensions of the bathroom which saves on further renovation costs.'

Soon after our sit down we went our separate ways but before I got back to the hospital, I had to get into my car. It suffices to say that transferring from a high level to a low level is certainly easier, than the other way round.

During my time in hospital I started to take an active interest in alternative herbal remedies. I focused my attention on two areas;

blood circulation and unwanted calcification. Given the lack of normal muscle-use in the extremities of the body, blood does not return to the heart as efficiently as it is sent to those extremities, so I decided a herbal response to assist a hastier return up the body was appropriate.

I also decided to take a natural remedy that brings about an increased durability to the cartilage of the joints, decreasing the opportunity for bones to damage each other.

About this time, the first fundraising event organised by my club was held in a local golf club. It was a golf classic where teams of four played against each other. Each tee was sponsored and the day ended with a three-course meal in the clubhouse.

During the meal an auction and raffle were held, the total of the proceeds exceeded any expectations I had, but more importantly the funds raised together with a local authority grant, were sufficient to bring about the adaptations necessary to the family home and pay off what I owed on the car. The organising committee had already decided that their next venture would be a major dinner at the Burlington Hotel in the city. Progress on both the fundraising and the rehabilitation fronts.

Given my progression in physiotherapy, it was decided that I would be a good candidate for leg braces or calipers. Calipers are the generic term given to devices that support the limbs, allowing them to function. Mine would be referred to as CAFHOS or calf, ankle, foot and hip orthopaedic supports.

The first thing to be done in designing a pair of CAFHOS is to take measurements of the patient's legs, then decide on the requisite amount of plaster of paris necessary to make moulds, from which the plastic moulds, with their entwined metal supports are made. I had a choice of colours – black, white, denim, rainbow or leopard. Since I felt angelic, white, plain denim, flower-power rainbow and jungle leopard skin were not quite me, that left black as my chosen colour. The manufacturer said he would return in about a month with the initial moulds of the leg braces and it would be another two weeks before the final product would be ready.

He decided against giving me any degree of flexion in the angle of the feet; instead he decided to keep the foot support at right angles to the ankle support. He felt this was appropriate given the tightened and flexed angle of my hips. Any further addition to this flexed angle could lock me into a stationary position making it very difficult to propel forward.

I believe I will walk again, I do not know when so I refuse to put a date on it… If it takes years, if it takes decades, it simply does not matter.

Thirteen

A Thought-Out Progression, Love Lost And Walking On

ONE afternoon I turned to my physiotherapist and asked him what he thought about the way things were going.

'Now that I've started with the leg braces how much use do you think I can get out of them?'

'Well I think you should try to get consistent use from them for the long term.'

'So if I use them everyday will the paralysis improve,' I asked.

'All I can say is if you use them every day the paralysis will not get worse, in the sense that your joints and in particular your hip joints will not atrophy. Using them in conjunction with your full range of stretching exercises will improve your flexibility and to some extent your mobility.'

'It's the prospect of improved mobility that drives me on,' I added.

'You must never forget how far you have already come. Remember the doctors at the first conference were pointing to transferring in and out of the chair and turning over in bed as the primary targets of your physiotherapy programme. That in my opinion was well below what you could achieve and you continue to prove me right.'

'And being in the pool now for hydrotherapy can only help?'

'Absolutely, yes.'

'Ok, there are things I'm doing in the water that I cannot do on land.'

'That would be true of most patients. It's the lack of gravity in the pool that helps.'

'Do improvements evident in the pool one day become apparent on land? In other words, is movement in the water a prediction of movement to come on the land?' I asked.

'No. I have patients who happen to have a great range of movement in the water but have hardly any movement when gravity is in play.'

'So it's probably better that the gap between land and water is not too wide.'

'Probably, though never forget each patient will vary.'

While clear progress was being made with physiotherapy, the same could not be said of another area of rehab, namely socialising with the opposite sex as a disabled man.

'There is no way any woman will find you attractive in a wheelchair,' said Fear.

'The omnipotent one has spoken, bow before the all-knowing one,' replied Faith.

'Joke all you like but you know there is truth in what I'm saying.'

'The women that see only the chair are the women I will want to avoid.'

'That will probably leave you with a select few to choose from.'

'I have always preferred quality to quantity.'

'Well, you're certainly bringing a whole new meaning to that phrase, as the sort of quality you're looking for is probably extinct. Then of course even if the miraculous does occur, there is that distinct lack of erectile function.'

'There are medications for that sort of thing.'

'Certainly, just imagine it, saintly woman because that's the sort of quality you'll need, is in a state of arousal and your response is, 'sorry babe it'll be another few hours before things start to look up'. Should do wonders for spontaneity.'

'Well that scenario if it happens within the context of a mutually loving relationship will not be a problem. Let me put it to you in words you'll understand, hardness will hardly be a problem.'

'Still what you are saying is predicated entirely on finding a very tolerant woman. Let's face it, a lot of frustration lies ahead. After all you are still attracted to women but your appeal for prospective partners has taken a noise dive.'

'Your opinion of women is very low. Confidence is a characteristic that women find appealing.'

'I agree but what confidence can you possibly have when you are half the man you were before?'

'I'm drawing confidence from within myself in a way I have not done before.'

'Oh, self-delusion, the final resting place on the path to self-destruction.'

'I draw confidence from the commitment I have made to physiotherapy and the improvements I continue to make. As I get the results I seek my confidence grows. These results are best seen over time, for example, on 11 February 2002 I had a flicker of a muscle movement around my right hip – one year later on 11 February 2003 I had a flicker of movement in both knees. While there is no guarantee that this recovery will continue there was no guarantee that the results to date would materialise either. But my confidence is not based entirely on my physical and mental response to the injury it is also based on my spiritual response to it.

That is to say, I believe I will walk again, I do not know when so I refuse to put a date on it. In other words, the depth of my commitment to a total recovery is such that I have completely removed time from the equation. If it takes years, if it takes decades, it simply does not matter.'

'Hate to spoil the party but the negative aspect to this approach is the difficulty in sharing a life that has become consumed by its dedication to itself.'

'That is a price I am prepared to pay.'

*   *   *

As time progressed, so too did my physiotherapy. One afternoon my therapist had another surprise for me, he produced a Zimmer frame.

'Is that for me?' I queried.

'Yes, it's time to try it out.'

'Just me, the splints, the frame and yourself.'

'That's all, nobody else.'

Once again, I found myself on the edge of the plinth, with my legs straight out in front of me, strapped up in the splints. Only this time there was less support than before. I made my customary grab for the frame which my physio held in place for me until I straightened up. My first attempt at swinging my leg from the hip proved unsteady but after a while I managed to recover my balance and tried again.

The second attempt resulted in an uncontrolled collapsing movement from my hip. This time my physio steadied me. My third attempt at a step proved to be my best. I managed to place my foot about 12 inches ahead of where it previously had been. Faltering and weak steps followed until I had covered a distance of about 10 metres. At this point I held onto the frame with what remaining strength I had before the physio placed my wheelchair behind me so I could fall back onto it.

I was practising with the Zimmer for a week before the first rumblings of going home were mooted. I had expected to go home in about a month to six weeks. I was not very satisfied with the timing of the would-be return for a number of reasons; firstly, out-patient status meant a reduction in the amount of time I would spend at therapy. It would be a change from three hours every day, Monday to Friday, down to two hours per week. Fifteen hours reduced to two – that's drastic.

Once home the possibilities for hydrotherapy would be severely limited, in addition, the house had not as yet been adapted to my needs and I did not have the necessary equipment to carry out physiotherapy at home. For me to gain proficiency with the leg braces I needed a plinth; for stretching, lying down and receiving electrical treatment, a mat; to park my chair for a stable base while doing weights for my arms and chest; parallel bars; a Zimmer frame and crutches to practise both standing and walking. While I still did not have the control or strength to walk with the crutches, they were something to aim for. Such an aim was not over stretching if my progress in the pool was anything to go by.

At that time, I was receiving hydrotherapy twice a week and I had started side of the pool crab walking. This is walking in a seated position as before, only doing so sideways and parallel to the wall of the pool. It was something that the physiotherapists thought I would not be able to do. However, I managed to do it without that much difficulty.

*Conditions were not right
for my return home while
conditions in rehab remained
conducive for further progress.*

Fourteen

The Stone And
The Transeva

IT was late October when I learned I had a calcium stone in my bladder. I went to Tallaght Hospital for an exploration of my bladder because of the number of infections I had been getting. The consultant discovered the stone and stated that it was the cause of the infections. This result was a surprise given that nothing showed up on an X-ray of my bladder, kidneys and urethra only three weeks earlier.

The stone could not be removed there and then and given its position and size it could not be broken down by a laser. Instead I was given a date in early December for its removal while under an anaesthetic. In a way I had hoped this would be the case because theoretically at least it would keep me in rehab for a slightly longer time. Conditions were not right for my return home while conditions in rehab remained conducive for further progress. Planning for going home and general discussion of progress to date was supposed to occur on the day of the trip to Tallaght but was postponed until the following week.

Tension was building for that upcoming conference. The doctor wanted me to stay home for two consecutive nights. However, from my point of view, this was difficult given the lack of toiletry facilities at home. Furthermore the decision was made not to send any nurse, or nurse's assistant to Tallaght Hospital to accompany me. Instead it was expected that my mother would fulfil that requirement. This presumed that my mother would be available to accompany me. As it turned out she had difficulty in re-arranging her day around my 96-year-old grandfather and it was very inconvenient, to say the least.

Another source of tension, was the 'pressure on beds' concept. This essentially places greater importance on future patients rather than current ones by freeing beds for those future patients to become current ones. Thus the ongoing cycle continues, at times without any apparent consideration for the patient who finds himself sent home still awaiting an operation.

For the conference we resorted to a strategy that proved successful. Basically my parents and I would go into the conference and state how unsafe it would be for me to go home not only in a month's time but at weekends as well, given that work on the renovations to the house were underway and it was now something of a building site.

I was fighting an uphill battle and the primary reason was the doctors' diagnosis. They still had me classified as a complete spinal injury. In their view, full recovery would not occur and I had been allowed enough if not too much rehabilitation time already. Besides that, a future patient was waiting in the wings to fill my bed.

One week after the discovery of the stone I had the conference. It was plain that the hospital authorities wanted me to go home sooner rather than later although they recognised that the house would be unsafe while renovations were ongoing. They requested a date by which the house would be fit for my return; we said four to six weeks. It was decided to have another conference three weeks later. By then a clearer time frame would emerge. However something far more important was decided that day – a change to my official diagnosis. The consultant as before chaired the meeting and spoke first. 'Your most recent Asia score shows a big improvement on your previous one. Given the improvement we are inclined to change your diagnosis.'

I was next to talk: 'In what way have you changed your view?'

'We are of the view that you have an incomplete spinal cord injury.'

That was the statement I thought most unlikely to come and I felt vindicated by it.

A much younger
version of me.

Above: Visiting the Aran Islands in the sunshine.

Left: On holiday in Biarritz.

Right:
A different
girlfriend and a
different time.

Above: Cycling on the spot in the kitchen.
Opposite page: Walking between the bars in the hall.

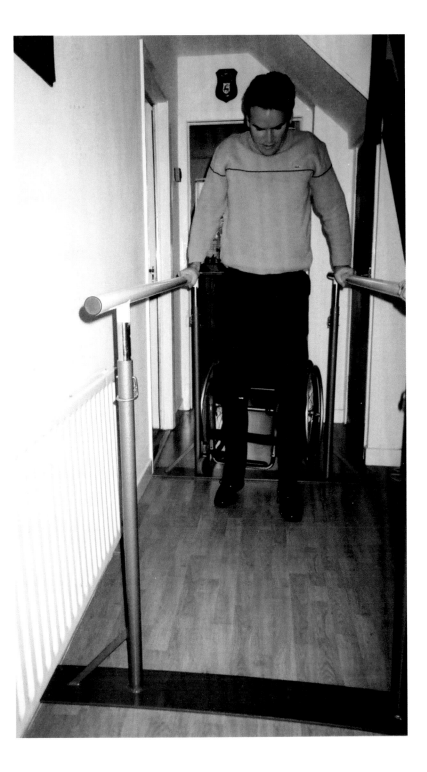

Above: Surrounded by family at my brother's wedding.
Below: With family at a fundraiser organised by CYM
Terenure in the Burlington Hotel with former Ireland
rugby captain Keith Wood in the background.

With my cousin Orla (above) and girlfriend Liz (below) soon after the injury.

Below: About to enjoy an Italian meal with my mother Brenda and brother Aidan.

With my thoughts in my back garden. Some day soon, I will sit here again, but I will then rise and I will walk alone.

'With the new diagnosis do you expect further improvement in the future?' I asked.

'I would not rule it out but you'll have to work very hard over an extended period of time.'

'The physical aspect of rehabilitation has never fazed me and I will remain committed to it for as long as is required.'

'I am convinced that you will.'

In fairness this consultant always treated me as person rather than an injury. Improvement to date and future improvement hinged on the various therapies I was receiving.

Aside from traditional physiotherapy with leg brace training and hydrotherapy, the third method of attempting to stimulate nerves is by electrical stimulus. I had not been exposed to such treatment but that all changed when a neighbour called to my family home with a magazine. It was a sports monthly and in it was an article on an electrical device called a 'Transeva'.

The originator of the device was a veterinary doctor. He discovered that with the right current and power muscle tears, ligament strains, cartilage damage and scar tissue will over time repair. He used his device to help animals in particular horses recover after injury. His device was not used on human patients; the reason being both the current and the power were too severe.

However a South African associate of the innovator adapted the device so that the current and power were of a sufficiently safe nature for human patients. It was first used on people there. It has since been utilised on a more widespread basis in the southern hemisphere and most recently in Britain and Ireland. There are a number of features that make the device unusual.

Firstly it can be applied to the area of injury directly. Virtually all other electrical aides cannot be. It imparts alternate current other aides utilise direct current. It breaks down scar tissue, the hardened tissue left after an area has suffered trauma, this tissue acts as an obstacle to deadened nerves that may otherwise have the capacity to return to normal functioning. Thus removal of this scar tissue is a direct help to recovery. Other electrical aides do not breakdown scar tissue.

The article provided information about the machine and it also gave a contact telephone number as well as an e-mail address. I made contact and one of the first requests made of me by the Transeva therapist was to provide her with information about the injury, the surgery and the treatment. She was based in England but conferred with her boss in South Africa and together they decided I was a suitable candidate for electrical treatment. In November the therapist came to Dublin.

'How many other paraplegics has the treatment benefited in terms of a total recovery?' I asked.

'It has been used to help 15 other paraplegics with differing degrees of success,' she explained.

'How long does the treatment last?'

'Forty minutes is the recommended duration for treatment in order to gain benefit.'

'How often can treatments occur?'

'Once every 48 hours.'

'What are the chances of the treatment helping me walk again?'

'Good when the treatments are carried out in conjunction with physio.'

'If we decide to go ahead, what treatment schedule do we initiate?'

'Normally patients with paralysis have the option to buy the machine and have someone close to them trained in its use so a schedule of once every second day can be carried out.'

For the first time since the incident I had spoken to people who had a positive outlook on my condition. I was hopeful but I was even more determined to control my expectations. When the therapist, who oversaw the Transeva's use in both Britain and Ireland came to Dublin, we arranged to have the first session one evening in the hospital. The therapist arrived with her husband.

As it happened they met as a consequence of her treating him with the electrical device. He had been a professional cricket player who sustained an injury that left him in constant pain. The treatment eradicated the pain and he had become an advocate for it ever since.

'Thanks for seeing me and I hope it will help,' I said.

'It will, with time you'll be able to see an improvement,' she said confidently.

'Could you explain the procedure to me as you go through it?'

'Certainly, the first thing to do is to prepare the electrical pads by steeping them in salty water. Then put gel on both pads.'

This took a few minutes during which she told me that many rugby players have been treated with the Transeva. I never did ask why the device is called a Transeva but I have always thought it has to do with its origins or more specifically the origins of its creator, Winks Greene. Winks hails from the Transvaal and modified the device so it could be used on human beings, perhaps she named it after her place of birth.

'Place the larger pad in direct contact with the skin, attach it to the control box and plug it into the mains. Then place the smaller pad with its handle on the injured area. Do not turn on the device until both the therapist and the patient are comfortable. Turn up the voltage knob slowly, do not lift the pad off the skin because to do so would give the patient an electric shock.'

'Ok, so far no shock.'

'Well, that's a relief.'

'Tell me what is your expectation for this first session?'

'I hope to see vibrations around your backside and if we get that it will be a good start.'

'So you want me to shake my ass,' I joked.

'That would be great... I am getting a reaction just here, and yes, it's more than just your backside that is reacting it's the back of your legs as well.'

This showed that not all nerves were dead and that the long process of breaking down the scar tissue had begun. So for me the only remaining issue was finding out if enough nerves had survived to allow a recovery.

Fifteen

Transeva Magic, House Renovations And The Stone's Removal

THE first treatment with the Transeva went well. In fact, it could not have gone any better. Not only was there a reaction from the backside and the hamstrings but also from the calves and the feet. This reaction was well beyond any expectations given that ordinarily getting a reaction from the feet takes many weeks if not months to achieve.

I told the physiotherapists about the device and they were very keen to hear more so I set up a meeting at which the Transeva therapist could explain to them the nature of the device. With excitement abounding it would be all too easy to misinterpret the Transeva as a magic solution to paralysis. It is not but in combination with all the other therapies it certainly does have a role to play – and a very positive role at that. In addition, while breaking down the scar tissue it also increases the strength in muscles that show any sign of life.

Work on the house began soon after I started treatment with the Transeva. One of the first concerns was the outlet for the gas, it had to be moved to allow work on the ramp at the front of the house to begin. It was moved to a higher position on the front wall of the house, thus allowing room for the ramp to be put in place.

Construction of the ramp also required the front door of the house to be lifted to a position where it would meet the end point of the ramp. The ramp itself starts at street level and rises with a gradient of 1 in 12. Running along the side of the ramp are railings. They were put in position for safety reasons when it is wet or frosty. The railings help with cautious movement. The lift to upstairs was installed within 48 hours and apparently it had to be installed prior to the work upstairs beginning in earnest.

Since my brother moved to Italy we had an empty bedroom available, so it was decided to reduce our five-bedroom to a four-bedroom house. The dividing wall between two of these bedrooms was removed and the smaller of the two rooms was converted into a bathroom that in turn became the ensuite of another bedroom. This ensuite bedroom became my room, a 'floating' wooden finished floor was laid in the room, allowing me to wheel the chair around the room very freely. The floor is referred to as floating because it is laid in such a way as to leave a gap between it and the original floor.

Similar floors were laid in the kitchen and hall, once again allowing freewheeling movement with minimum shoving from me. Shelves and a completely made over wardrobe were added to the bedroom. A video and television as well as a sliding door to separate the bathroom from the bedroom added further to a tastefully finished room.

As all these changes to the house were ongoing, my final conference was called for the middle of November.

'Your various rehab programmes are now complete. Mindful of this, discharge from the hospital is imminent,' I was told.

'How soon is imminent?' I asked.

'Once the arrangements are in place, I would say, days.'

'But as you know the house is not safe for me to return.'

'We are aware of that, so we are implementing hospital policy as it applies in a situation such as this. We are initiating a patient swap.'

'What exactly does that entail?'

'We return you to the hospital from where you came and that hospital sends us a more acute patient than yourself.'

'The house is likely to be ready in two weeks. Does that factor in at all?'

'Once programmes have ended we have no choice but to set the policy in motion.'

'In effect, it means over a two-week period I will spend time in three hospitals. This one, my previous one and the one for the removal of the stone,' I said.

As it turned out, policy implementation was not possible. My previous hospital, the Mater Hospital was not receiving patients at that time due to a lack of available beds and a vomiting bug that meant both patients and visitors were being turned away. Instead, I stayed another two weeks in rehab before going to Tallaght Hospital for my bladder stone removal.

I finished my treatments in rehab a week before I was due to get my stone removed – I had a 'rest' week. That was something I was not happy with because I knew while in hospital before the stone's removal and indeed for a good while after, I would not be in any position to do physiotherapy. So I was looking at a period of six weeks if not longer of no physical treatment.

It would be easier to accept this forced inactivity if I was convinced it was doing something for me; but I firmly believed otherwise. Physiotherapy is the primary example of me taking action that is best for me; it is both my duty and desire. I know I can improve by doing physio. Bladder and bowel are unlike physio in that I can control them but not improve them or push them any closer to normality. With physio, while, I have no promise of a return to normality, I can at least push some of the way. Removing physio from my routine felt like a direct assault on my 'raison d'etre'.

My kidney stone was removed on a Tuesday and I returned home the following Saturday. The consultant was a little disappointed that he did not discover a source to the infection that led to the over-production of calcium that had led to the formation of a stone.

Usually a foreign body like a hair is the root cause but not in this instance. Given that there was no clearly specified cause the chances are that calcium stones could become an ongoing problem. The regular use of the Transeva makes that possibility less likely since its electrical impulses have the capacity to break up stones before they become too obstructive.

Sixteen

Returning Home

MY return home was not in the slightest bit traumatic. Instead it felt like a most natural progression. The work on the house adaptations had reached a point where all the changes had been made and my room was fully functional – only the décor remained to be done. It was being carried out in conjunction with the overall decorative changes to the house that had just begun when I returned home.

Life was beginning to move in a more pleasant direction again. Returning to work full-time in January would not be very constructive without a staggered re-familiarisation with the routine that had been a very central aspect of my life. So on two consecutive Fridays I went into work and began to get a feel for the old routine once again.

What surprised me was the reaction I got not only from work colleagues but from people who hardly knew me. They were delighted to see me and ceaselessly voiced their best wishes for my future. I think the main reason for people's positive approach to me was their view that I lacked bitterness. To some extent that happens to be true; nevertheless there are times when the fear within me asserts itself or at least tries.

'They're only nice to you because they think you're putting on a false front,' said Fear.

'They're only nice to me because they see me trying to restore normality to my life,' replied Faith.

'Still if you stayed away from rugby completely you would not be in a chair.'

'It appears that way but there is no point trying to live life free of risk.'

'No just free of rugby.'

'Well I do not feel bitter about playing rugby again after the time I spent away from it.'

'Of course not and I'll bet you have no regret either.'

'Bitterness no, regret, yes.'

Seventeen

New Year, Promotional Activity And New Hope

IT was time for the vigil mass on Christmas Eve; as a family we were ready to go to the chapel. I had not been to a Christmas Eve mass in many years. Instead the dawn mass on Christmas Day in a different parish was my preferred option. However this year, such an option was not available, the reason being I was not sure if I had direct access to that church. For the first time in my life, access to buildings had become a personal issue. It was my first Christmas in a wheelchair.

We arrived at the Vigil Mass in plenty of time. The chapel is located on the grounds of my old school. Memories came to mind of time spent playing rugby and winning championships on the running track. Sitting there in the chapel, did I feel broken at a time when the Christian message to the world is one of great joy and universal peace?

No, I did not feel broken, I felt relaxed with the divine spirit within me and at one with my family. Did I feel anguished, bitter or resentful this first Christmas wheeling rather than walking? No, I had none of those feelings. So at an emotional level this particular Christmas was not any different from any other that preceded it. Something that may not be readily believable but nevertheless remains true. The meaning of Christmas for me is unchanged, living through love to experience both joy and peace.

After Mass I was making my way to the exit when something unique took place. A few old teachers of mine said hello, shared season's greetings and cried for me. It was the first time they had seen me in my paralysed state. I could see the sadness and sympathy in their eyes. These people were moved to tears. Not floods of tears, but reluctant tears, reluctant to show how upset they were in case they upset me. Caring, thoughtful teachers touched in a way that elevated their humanity.

I left the chapel, got into my car and drove us all home. During my stay in Rehab I was learning to get the most from my broken body while at the same time retaining an unbroken spirit. One of the lessons learned was to be patient with my condition, have the discipline to remove my urgent desire for an immediate restoration of my physical state.

Thankfully that Christmas lacked any urgency; instead it provided me with a belief that life beyond rehabilitation was worth living. New Year's Day was also my first in a wheelchair. My brother and his wife along with my mother were standing over me as I lay on the plinth. The design of the plinth is such that it allows a person to lay face down without having to turn their head to the side. Everyone was a little nervous including myself.

'Ok, I have gelled the pads placed one underneath you and am about to place the other onto your back,' said my mom.

'Don't turn on the machine until the pad is in contact with the skin or else you'll shock me.'

'I know, the pad is touching the skin now so I'll keep it there as I turn on the current. Now, do you feel anything?'

'Not yet.'

'Ok, how about now?'

'You must have turned it up because I'm beginning to feel it now.'

'There, did you feel that?'

'Yes, I'm getting a kicking movement which is going all the way down to the feet.'

Just as my mother told me what was happening my brother and his wife started to cheer and hold onto my hands. The current continued to go through me for the next 40 minutes.

'It seems to be stronger above the injury near the top of the scar,' said my brother.

'Well that's to be expected, I don't feel a kick at the centre of the scar where most of the damage is.'

'You don't feel it because it's not happening at least not to the same extent as above or below the scar. There is a slight flicker of movement shooting through the backside but it's not going down the legs.'

With the passing of time even the most traumatised area responded better to the current passing through it. Within a week of my first treatment with my own Transeva, I was back at work. My aim was to mix a full return to work with a full workload of physiotherapy. Given the flexible work hours I could mix both. A working day for me starts with the radio alarm reminding me it's 5. 30am and time to wake up.

Ablutions and dressing that once took 20 minutes now take a full hour, so by 6.30am, I'm at breakfast. I usually have breakfast with my mother who has already come in from her three and a half mile walk. By seven with the morning paper read I get into my car and head into work. The office, at that hour, with the traffic light, is only 20 minutes away.

On that first day, like each working day since, I drove into an underground car park and parked in a reserved spot. Prior to the injury, parking was away from the workplace and never a certainty. Once I transferred from the car into the chair I took a lift up to my office, it was 7.30am and time for work. There I was back at my desk about to start a job that had been kept for me through my father's diligence and my employer's desire to retain me. My duties were familiar yet fresh on that first day, when just being there was all that mattered.

Aside from work and physiotherapy a third activity had entered my life and unlike the other two it was totally new to me: promotional work. The organising committee of the rugby club advised me that given the magnitude of the planned Gala Dinner at the end of March, I would need to give interviews with the media in order to promote the event.

Apart from the newspaper and radio interviews I was contacted by the national television broadcaster, RTÉ and they asked me to appear on a live afternoon show. It was further exposure, the sort that would help a great deal. What made the television interview a little different from the other interviews was the reference made to acceptance of my situation. My response to which was when the injury first occurred, I thought to myself that I would never walk again, it was also the last time I've had that thought. In other words, I have not accepted my situation as a 'fait accompli'.

Soon after the television interview I started out-patient physiotherapy at the Rehab. The initial period of physio would last six to eight weeks and it would be followed by an assessment. The primary objective of the physio would be standing balance. This is being able to stand with the support of the leg braces and nothing else. The standing balance objective, once achieved, would allow better quality assisted walking to take place for longer durations.

The promotional/fundraising aspect of my life was not only new but certainly the most surprising. For example, when the president of the Past Pupils Union of my old school rang up asking if it would be acceptable to send on a cheque to the Ciarán McCarthy fund, needless to say I did not object nor did I object to former classmates organising a fundraising lunch down at the Terenure Rugby Club. The lunch coincided with the Ireland versus Wales rugby match and was held in conjunction with a raffle/auction.

That was an event I will never forget because of one single act of pure generosity. A schoolmate with whom I had lost contact – in fact the previous time I had seen him was nine years earlier at a school reunion – made a bid for a jersey worn by an Irish international. The jersey was worth no more than €80 or €90. It was bought for €3,600. Afterwards I told the buyer that it was totally unnecessary. All he said was he'd like to think I would do the same for him had the situation been reversed. This single act brought into clear focus the goodwill I was receiving from many different quarters.

The Past Pupils Union was another source of funding. A letter from the president of the Union explained how the Benevolent Fund is sustained by charity and raffle events. Each year worthy causes associated with the school and past pupils are selected and supported according to greatest need. I was selected this year. This donation and the fundraising lunch were examples of the completely unsolicited support directed towards me and these instances generated a sense of awe.

It was a particularly sensitive time given the fact that one year had passed since the injury had taken place but as I hinted it was an anniversary lacking negative impact. Instead January 27, 2003 passed off much like the day before and the day after without incident. I did not dwell on that rainswept day the year before because my life since then had a renewed sense of purpose with a driving desire to recover. While the doctors continued to rate my chances as minimal, I focused on improvements, small but clearly evident. A timely improvement came within two weeks after that first anniversary.

It was another first anniversary that of my very first flicker of movement and to mark this I tried to push my feet forward while in the seating position. I managed to do so with my left but not the right. The movement emanated completely from the knee and quadriceps rather than the foot however this was further proof that nerve impulses were now being received further down the spine than before.

Balancing while in the standing position is a function associated with the nerves of sacral vertebrae one and two. The current belief in medicine is that restoration of sensation and movement in an ordered fashion down the spine is the desired recovery rather than a situation where the patient can move their toes but cannot move their knees. Such skipping can lead to an unfinished recovery and no more. This phenomenon was pointed out to me early on and it helped me realise the importance of knowledge and how it can influence hope. In short, true knowledge eradicates false hope whereas incomplete knowledge causes false hope to flourish. While hope is precious, it is also fragile so it should always be handled with care. Every now and then hope comes under scrutiny and discovering the Transeva and the potential it provides for improvement is an example. The hope is I will improve yet if and when an improvement occurs it is the overall effort of physiotherapy, hydrotherapy, reflexology and the Transeva that will bring it about and not any single activity.

The danger is to believe there is a miracle cure capable of solving my incapacity swiftly and efficiently when realistically at present there is not. Such a dangerous belief equates to false hope, yet one day a cure may indeed be available. So striving to maintain a balance between these two scenarios remains my greatest challenge.

Eighteen

Insurance, Neurology, The Dinner And Progressing Physiotherapy

IN early March, I got a call from the insurers who wanted the consultant's report so they could pay what was owed to me. My solicitor had been seeking medical reports from my various consultants. Eventually we were supplied with one from my rehabilitation consultant and a second from my orthopaedic consultant. The orthopaedic surgeon maintained that in his opinion it is unlikely I would ever walk again whereas the rehabilitation consultant was more circumspect yet not more optimistic.

Soon after receiving the opinion of the man who performed the surgery, the legal advice was followed and that was to pass the report on to the insurers. Within a month of receiving the written opinion of the surgeon the insurance was paid in full. This payment gave me a great deal of satisfaction simply because it was money that was owed unlike the charitable donations that were unsought after bonuses. Progress on the insurance front was matched by physio progress.

For the first time electrical impulses were been sent by the Transeva down both legs all the way to the feet from all along the scar. Previously, only from some areas of the scar would the impulses travel all the way down to the feet not at every point along the scar. This was an improvement and more specifically, it signified a breaking down of the scar tissue at the site of the trauma. Electrically induced progression occurred in conjunction with a significant neurological advance as well.

My knees were showing signs of life. I found that I could sit at the edge of the plinth and kick my feet forward. The very initial sign of life in the knees occurred on February 11. At that stage I could flick my feet forward then some six weeks later I could kick a football with a swing of each foot.

Something that was gaining forward momentum was preparation for the gala dinner and my promotional work had become an important part of my day-to-day activity. The dinner proved to be very successful and was held two days before the Grand Slam decider against England. It was only the seventh time in Irish rugby history that the Irish team were involved in a match that if they won would secure a clean sweep of victories in the championship. A feat they managed to do on only two previous occasions.

That afternoon my brother travelled from Italy with his wife and brother-in-law and stayed for the weekend. For me having them there was a true delight. He is a fan of rugby as much as I am so the evening was a treat for him as well. My other brother was looking forward to rubbing shoulders with a few famous players.

The dinner was the first time that the 1985 Irish rugby team was publicly feted. I never did find out why this was the case but felt honoured they agreed to come along. On the night, the team were all there with the exception of two who could not attend due to work commitments. The evening began with a champagne reception where the selected few mingled with the Triple Crown team.

This was followed by the dinner itself. For the main course we had a choice of beef or brille. The brille was served in a mango sauce and finished with a slice of banana. During the meal a presentation of engraved Waterford glass was made to each of the players and a video of their historical achievement was run on three large screens. Our compere for the evening kept to a steady schedule with the meal coming to an end around 11 o'clock.

At that point, there was an interview with two commentators from the BBC: an Irishman who captained both his country and the Lions touring team, Keith Wood and an Englishman who, before he retired from the game, was regarded as a central midfield player of the highest quality, Jeremy Guscott. These two were asked their opinion on current issues in the game as well as their views on the upcoming grand slam decider between England and Ireland where needless to say partisanship won through.

Their interview was followed by my thank you speech. I said that the evening was cause for celebration in two ways. The first was a personal celebration in that the proceeds raised that night would help me acquire and adapt a house suitable to my needs. Something that would not at all be possible without the hard work, efficient organisation and true commitment of the committee set up by my rugby club CYM Terenure. So on my own behalf and on that of my family I expressed our heartfelt gratitude.

The second cause for celebration was the feat of the Triple Crown-winning Irish team of 1985. Beating England, Scotland and Wales as this team did was a rare achievement and had not been repeated in the 18 years since. Finally, I thanked everyone for being there and wished one and all an enjoyable evening.

For the speech I decided not to mention my recovery to date. While I am certainly proud of my recovery I thought those who turned up expected to see a former rugby player in a wheelchair not a former rugby player about to stand up and do his imitation of Michael Flatley's Lord of the Dance. While dancing was not yet feasible, physiotherapy was continuing both at home and at rehab.

I was in the gym of the rehabilitation hospital, as an out-patient, with my leg braces on, sitting in my chair between the parallel bars, waiting for my physio to approach. As she came over I saw that she had crutches in her hands.

'Hi, I'm already to go, who are the crutches for?' I asked.

'They're for you,' she replied.

'Do you think I'm ready?'

'Well we're about to find out.'

'It's a big jump. After all, it means making the progression from six point walking to four point walking.'

'A physiotherapist could not have said it better. So much for the theory now is the time to do it.'

At that time, the first half of my physiotherapy sessions concentrated on stretching and preparing the body to stand. The second half concentrated on standing and walking. To stand up I grab the parallel bars. Then I elevate myself into a standing position by using my arms on the bars. Once up in the standing position I stretch out the pelvis and the base of the back and practise achieving standing balance.

'Ok, take the crutches and maintain standing balance, then once you're comfortable go for a few steps.'

'I don't think I'll ever be comfortable in this position but it does beat the hell out of the chair.'

'Are you ready?' she asked.

I nodded.

'Right, just remember while stepping technique is important more specifically shifting weight distribution from one side of the body to the other is key. The idea is to keep the body weight on the side of the body that is not taking the step that way 'the stepping side' has minimum weight to carry as the leg hitches forward. This technique is helped by correctly positioning the crutches with the lead crutch acting as a pivot for the side of the body taking the weight.'

Then came the first step, with the crutches almost planted in the ground from the immense strain I was putting through them. With my body slightly stooped my arms were sore from the effort of standing and were tiring fast.

Nevertheless my left leg hitched hesitantly forward and then stopped. My balance was good so I shifted my weight to the left side of my body and repeated the hitched step with my right leg.

I progressed this way for about four metres, stopped and collapsed backwards once the physio wheeled my chair into position behind me.

I was delighted to have walked in this way because when the injury first occurred 12 months earlier, it was very difficult to envisage any movement of any kind.

The hydro-therapist was very pleased with my progress and she suggested I continue the 'hydro' sessions in a pool closer to home.

Nineteen

Cycling

IT was a cold damp November afternoon and I was about to have my last hydrotherapy session in the national rehabilitation pool. Two years had passed since I left the hospital at the end of my nine-month initial stay. I had without doubt improved in the low gravity water environment. With the buoyancy of the water and the bar at the side of the pool, for balance, I could squat up and down in the water. In addition, while I was not absolutely straight when I stood by the side of the pool, the fact remains …I stood.

The hydro-therapist was very pleased with my progress and she suggested I continue the 'hydro' sessions in a pool closer to home. My view was at variance with hers as I did want to continue the hydro sessions except between sustained intervals of more traditional physiotherapy. It and the combination of reflexology and electrical treatment were the reasons for my standing in the pool.

She accepted my view: 'Certainly the work you have been doing is paying off but the pool is a unique environment allowing you greater opportunities to move.'

'I would like to return to the water but how long is the current waiting list for this pool?'

'About eight months, but if you arrange an out-patient check-up asking for a few hydro sessions, you could probably cut that waiting time in half.'

'OK, but there is one thing I need to ask you, can you arrange a time with out-patients for me to come in and try the exercise bicycles?'

'I can do that but cycling would be a big challenge.'

'Well I think I could do it or more to the point I would like the chance to try.'

'I'll talk to the out-patient physiotherapist and ask her to give you a call.'

The call came about four weeks later with an appointment to soon follow. Arriving at rehab, I was both nervous and excited about the possibility of cycling. Quite apart from the fact that even in the whole of my health I very rarely cycled, if I was to do it now it would open up the potential for strengthening my legs in a very progressive way.

It would allow me to set targets for increasing not only strength but stamina as well. Of course both of these much coveted objectives depended on being able to turn the pedals without any help. I would soon find out if that was possible.

The outpatient physiotherapist was older than the hydrotherapist and was very experienced. She was equally constructive in her approach maintaining that we should start with the exercise bicycles in the sports hall.

The layout of the rehabilitation hospital is such that it spreads out over a wide area with the building itself not exceeding four storeys at its highest point. It takes less than two minutes to get from the main physiotherapy gym to the sports hall. Once you enter the sports hall you find yourself on a basketball court that is used for many different sports such as table tennis, archery, shooting and occasionally bowls. Off to the right hand side of the court is a specially adapted weights room for wheelchair users. It is in this room that the exercise bikes are located. Once one was chosen, the precarious transfer from chair to bike began.

While the weights room has specially adapted weight machines, the exercise bikes are not adapted. The thinking behind this is that the vast majority of wheelchairs users, specifically spinal cord injury patients, are not in a position to use them. Anyway, with the help of two people I transferred from my chair to the bike. Once I found my balance on the bike and with my feet on the pedals I tried to cycle. It proved frustrating.

Firstly, my feet were not secure on the pedals, the power in my legs simply did not go all the way to my toes. Secondly, the power I did have was not enough to complete a full rotation of the pedals, leaving me unhappy with what was happening. While I was attempting to move the pedals around the physiotherapist was looking closely at the movement I did have. She thought if my backside had greater support I could probably rotate the pedals as the standard design of a saddle left too much body weight for my legs to carry.

Mindful of this change in emphasis she brought me to the occupational therapy department where two exercise bikes with 'chair-like' saddles were still in use after they had first been introduced to rehab back in the very early days of its inception.

Once I had been transferred from my chair to the bike I noticed two differences straight away; greater support and my feet were far more secure on the pedals because they were firmly strapped on, unlike previously where loose ties proved insufficient.

I leaned slightly back and forced my left leg forward and down which brought a little purchase from the pedals. This was followed by a slight pause and then, I repeated the forward and down movement initially with only the left leg but then followed by the right leg as well. The rocking motion now coming from both legs steadily increased until I managed to rotate the pedals for an entire revolution. One full turn was followed by a second and a third and so on until I had completed six full rotations of the pedals. I felt delight and vindication; delighted with the state of my leg power and vindicated in my belief that it was more than possible, it was real.

The advice given to me by the physio was straightforward; keep doing it as much as you possibly can preferably on a daily basis, build it into your routine and increase the duration and workload steadily. Christmas was coming when I sat on the plinth with a bicycle husk at my feet. What a wonderful present it would be to cycle.

Once my feet were tied into the cycle shoes, I tried to cycle but to no avail. I could hardly get any movement from the pedals at all. A number of constraints became immediately apparent. Firstly, the heels of my shoes were bumping against the ground anytime I attempted to move the pedals. Secondly, there was a slight resistance in the pedals as I tried to turn them, something that my legs were not strong enough to take. Finally the power in my upper legs was not being brought into play while sitting on the plinth.

I had the bike brought to the bicycle shop to alter the positioning of the cranks so that the cycle shoes were more elevated than they had been to prevent contact with the ground. As it turned out it was more convenient to raise the entire back end higher rather than the cranks alone. A rubber band connecting the drive wheel with the fly wheel was removed which effectively removed all resistance from the pedals.

My third difficulty was proving more obdurate than the rest. The shape of the 'chair-seat' on the bike in rehab was not easily duplicated and apart from my upper leg strength not getting through, I was also giving myself friction sores on my backside from using the plinth as a seat.

The shape of the 'chair-seat' was akin to a baler's seat on a harvesting machine, where two hollows in the seat allowed space for the upper legs to move freely. However balers' seats are not that readily available; nonetheless, one day a moment of true inspiration hit and it was decided to place the cushion from my wheelchair on top of the plinth. It had the desired double effect of no friction and free movement. With the adaptations complete I started to cycle confident in the knowledge that a clearly-defined progression of improvement was distinctly possible.

Since I had the resistance removed from the bike I could work on establishing some stamina in the legs. The plan was to establish stamina over a six-month period, then change the emphasis to improving strength by re-introducing resistance in the pedals. I started in January 2005 three years after my last rugby match and by June I could rotate the pedals 600 times. Three hundred times forward, allowing the muscles in the front of the legs to work and 300 times backwards, working the backs of the legs: all rotations being completed within 20 minutes. The resistance introduced in June was comparable to a middle gear of a ten-speed bike. Within six weeks, cycling backwards as well as forwards was just starting to become possible.

In April, my six-month check-up with the surgeon was due so I wanted him to see how things were progressing. Instead of attempting to bring the bike into the outpatients' waiting room of the hospital which would prove difficult, it was decided to use a camcorder. So in we went, my father and myself, to the hospital. Not for the first time that visit was to prove a watershed. I have always enjoyed my visits with the surgeon primarily because he responds positively to patients who are constructive when handling their affliction.

Conversations with him usually started with the question, what have you got for me? 'We have something to show you,' I said.

My father then showed the surgeon a recording of me sitting on the plinth cycling away.

'He's only just starting to move the pedals.'

'Yes, but he is moving them.'

'Now he's cycling. There is no resistance.'

'No need for resistance.'

'He wants it and hopes to introduce it in the next few months.'

The surgeon turned away from the camcorder and sat down, after a pause he asked: 'Can you stand?'

'Yes, with the aid of leg braces and the middle finger of my left hand.'

'What about without leg braces?' he questioned.

'No.'

'What area is letting you down when you try to stand?'

'The upper hamstring on my left side is tending to give way.'

'That would be your extensor muscles.'

'Would the cycling improve the extensors?'

'It could, but you need to stand before you can walk.'

I was pleased, the man who operated on me was finally discussing the possibility of walking but I wanted to move the conversation in a different direction.

'What about all the fine work that is been done on stem cell research, do you see any grounding breaking news there?'

'Not for another 10 perhaps 20 years, the current work is progressing at the micro-biological level but more importantly no work is being done on primates. Without the primate work, experimental procedures on humans is not going to happen.'

'But you were satisfied that I needed the operation you performed?'

'From a medical viewpoint, a decision had to be made regarding your operation. When you were brought into the hospital you had what is called spinal shock, it is not always appropriate to operate in those conditions, so it comes down to an informed yet partially instinctual decision by the surgeon, in your case greater damage could have occurred without the procedure.'

'Such damage would have been a complete severing of the cord.'

'What we call a trans-section, yes. But let me remind you, your damage was equivalent to a trans-section.'

'You saw the damage, you know what it was like perhaps better than anyone. On the day you opened me up and looked inside would you have said I would one day cycle like you have just seen on tape?'

Nothing was said for a few moments then he replied: 'No, I would not.'

There it was – the response I had hoped to bring about. The implication was huge; I had defied medical expectation and joined an elite group, one of the three percent who regain functional movements after the equivalent of a complete injury to the spinal cord.

Twenty

Reality

'IT'S over three years now and the paralysis is as constant as it was at the beginning. Sure there has been minor improvements but nothing to change that status of wheelchair bound disability', said Fear.

'I do not believe the improvements have been minor especially considering the medical expectation from the outset was 'slim to no chance of walking again' and transferring into and out of the chair should be the physio target', replied Faith.

'Ok, let's assume these minor improvements continue, walking is still unlikely.'

'Walking will happen, time is the only issue.'

'Once again assuming you are correct, how long do the doctors give for the nerves within the spinal cord to make a recovery specifically the nerves that are still in tact?'

'The current medical view is two years but this view should not be regarded as 'de facto' especially when the feats of Christopher Reeve are considered. About seven years after his injury occurred he regained partial movement in his finger. This was completely unexpected but proved how time constraints should not be misinterpreted as limitations to recovery.'

'Nerves are only one part of the equation muscles are another consideration altogether. What is the life expectancy of unused muscles?'

'If muscles go unused for a period of about seven years it is unlikely that they will fully recover or recover at all. This fact points to the necessity of engaging paralysed limbs in some form of physical therapy, whether that means traditional physiotherapy, hydrotherapy, electrical treatment or some combination thereof. Irrespective of the chosen therapy or combinations of therapies what remains essential is carrying out a physical activity to stimulate the muscles.'

'How long should an individual continue physical therapy without regaining use of his limbs?'

'The good doctor will leave that decision to his patient. The average doctor will be caught up in putting time limits on his patients. My own view is that muscles should be stimulated well into the distant future because no one is in a position to know what possible medical advance may occur in the future. In addition, if nerves start showing signs of life but muscles have wasted, then the frightening scenario of having the potential to walk is lost because the muscle activity was never given enough consideration.'

'How long does it take to walk again?'

'Given the fact that damage to cords vary from injury to injury, the time to recover completely will vary from person to person. However doctors maintain that it takes up to two years for the swelling caused by the trauma to go away. Only then can a recovery, partial or otherwise, begin to occur.'

'If you believe you will walk again, when do you think it will be?'

'I don't believe in putting a time frame on walking again and generally I will not do so but it is a question that one-day will be answered in a definitive way. Given this inevitability I could speculate about a time frame without committing to it.

I believe that to commit to a time frame is to detract from an open ended commitment to physiotherapy – something which I will not allow to happen. So purely on a speculative basis, I believe I will walk again, with the best-case scenario being four years after the incident. This is predicated on my current rate of recovery continuing. The worse case scenario is to walk within 15 years after the incident and this particular possibility is predicated on not regressing from my current state of recovery.

Not regressing means maintaining any movement, sensation and muscle mass that I have and is something that necessitates physiotherapy for a long time to come. It is currently maintained within medicine that given the present rate of research stem cell operations will only have become mainstream and moved beyond their 'experimental treatment' label 15 years from now.'

'When all is said and done, you cannot deny the paralysis and the consequent labels of disabled, crippled and wheelchair bound for life,' said Fear.

'I deny nothing, but you seem to be missing the design destiny has settled on,' said Faith.

'Are you trying to tell me this whole experience is not about walking?'

'It's about an unrelenting will not to surrender to circumstances. Such fortitude of will is a by-product of faith or you could say it's a by-product of being me. You, as Fear, are losing your battle with me precisely because you cannot produce anything other than yourself. Fear begets fear whereas Faith begets hope. Therefore the growth of Fear is limited in a way that Faith is not.'

Once this realisation dawned on me, the internal conversation between Faith and Fear came to an end.

By seeing the condition of paraplegia as a permanent state whereby no functional improvements can ever be expected... doctors miss the individual patient's constructive attempts to improve their medical status

Twenty-one
Unwanted Calcium

F ROM early on in my rehabilitation, I developed the habit of daily physiotherapy. It required making a commitment whereby a mixture of discipline, determination and belief would see me reach my goal of total recovery from paraplegia. Needless to say there were occasions when I was convinced that belief in my recovery left me in a minority of one. This feeling of isolation was brought home to me when I met doctors and whatever their speciality was, their attitude tended to be the same.

The vast majority I met saw the 'condition' – not the patient. It was and remains an attitude not limited to just doctors but to a very broad spectrum of people. I simply expect more from medical professionals.

By seeing the condition of paraplegia as a permanent state whereby no functional improvements can ever be expected or where neurological return is not possible, doctors miss the individual patient's constructive attempts to improve their medical status.

To this day I find it disappointing but not surprising when encountering this causal preconceived notion that paralysis is for life and the best thing to do is accept it. Well my response is I do accept that I am in a wheelchair and all its incumbrances but I do so for today and only today. Not for tomorrow – in fact never tomorrow.

As time passed from January 27, 2002 on towards April 2008 my left leg was causing me difficulty. Specifically my left quadriceps were contracting to the extent that straightening my leg was no longer feasible since it had become kinked at a 35 degree angle. The implication for me was that physio was no longer improving my situation. At best a plateau had set in and assisted walking had become difficult.

After an appointment with my surgeon, he scheduled surgery for April 21. Removal of calcified material from my left hip and femur was to eradicate the bend in my leg and allow full extension. Medically it is unknown why some paraplegics/quadriplegics develop excessive calcium around their joints and bones while other paralysis sufferers do not.

A sizeable amount of calcium deposits was removed, two bucketfuls... though the size of those buckets remains a mystery. The stay in Cappagh Hospital lasted a week during which time I was sent to St Luke's Hospital for a targeted session of radiation. Post operative radiation on a decalcified area tends to prevent excessive calcium deposits from developing in the future. Not all calcium deposits were removed from my pelvic area but enough to free up the joint. As May became November, the calcification removal proved ineffective as the kink returned to my leg.

The surgeon maintained that a second concern had arisen after the operation about the scar tissue. It needed to be released if my leg was to ever straighten again. So surgery was pencilled in for November and in the run up to it my emotions were on the upswing again. The annoyance and frustration of a failed procedure to straighten my leg was replaced with the relief and joy of expecting a positive outcome this time around – but my buoyancy was soon to encounter a storm.

Twenty-two

Scar Tissue

THE operation to release the left quadriceps was planned for November 25, 2008. At that time standing with the assistance of the parallel bars and the leg braces was doable. It had become too difficult to walk with the braces and crutches around the kitchen table. It had become painful to carry out an exercise that had been built up patiently over the years since leaving the rehab in 2002. For the first time in six years my physiotherapy was regressing. My hips had always been very arthritic but this was the first occasion that they had become truly obstructive to my physiotherapy.

Admission to Theresa's ward at Cappagh National Orthopaedic Hospital was on November 24. The operation was straight forward and due to take place the next morning. It went ahead as planned and I returned to the ward that afternoon. Within 48 hours of the operation pyrexia, (high temperature), was evident as was a rapid heart rate, shortness of breath and rigors.

Rigors is when a person starts to shiver while at the same time their body temperature rapidly increases. It was then decided to move me to St. Anthony's Ward. This was the hospital's designated infection ward where within three weeks the symptoms had stabilised and I was allowed to return home for Christmas.

Leaving the hospital with a VAC machine attached to my leg was a first. A VAC device is a mechanised dressing designed to assist in the healing process. It is a battlefield innovation, invented and first utilised by the American military during their invasion of Afghanistan at the turn of the millennium. It applies negative pressure to a wound whereby a sucking action draws the flesh together. Christmas that year was a fairly subdued affair without our planned trip to visit my brother and his wife in Italy. Instead of northern Italy two and sometimes three trips to the hospital in northern Dublin had become the norm. The dressing needed to be changed regularly to be effective. However by the third week in January acute infection had returned again, only this time it proved to be life threatening.

Soon after my readmission to Cappagh, the surgeon approached both myself and my family. He told us that during the course of the operation the joint capsule of the left hip tore. Normally the fluid contained within would drain down and out the body. In my case this did not occur instead the fluid drained across the groin towards the post-operative wound sight.

Twenty-three

From Hospital
To Hospital

C LINICALLY I was not improving and it was decided that I should be transferred to the Mater Hospital. As a general hospital my surgeon believed that he could utilise a wider variety of specialists to address what had become a systemic blood infection or sepsis.

Once again I found myself in the National Spinal Unit where I had been in 2002 after the initial spinal trauma. The unit is the equivalent of an intensive care unit with both a nurse and doctor present at all times for a total of six patients. Blood was taken on a daily basis to measure the level of infection and to see how the system was managing to cope.

During those first few days of February, I was not always conscious but I remember being told by the microbiologist that the IV antibiotics being given to me were the strongest available and she hoped they would be sufficient. She also said that while the situation was grave, my system had shown some resilience.

I was dying but if I managed to survive a crucial 48-hour period after the antibiotics were pumped into me, then I would have stabilised and my life would no longer be in any immediate danger. The medication worked and I slowly started to improve.

Before leaving the Mater, a 'flap' operation to close the wound was undertaken. Such an operation is carried out by a plastic surgeon. In my case borrowed tissue from my stomach was transplanted to the left hip wound site in order to seal it. While the wound was finally closed continual systemic illness was evident and an IV drug was administered in heavy doses twice daily. The flap operation was my sixth operation involving a general anaesthetic in the 10-month period from April 2008 to February 2009.

To recap the operations;

April 2008: Calcification removal; to restore mobility;

November 2009: Soft tissue release; to ensure mobility;

December 2008–January 2009: Three wash-outs and debriding (removal of infected or dead tissue from wound sites) of the left hip;

February 2009: Flap to seal the wound.

I had endured a difficult period having undergone a high number of operations within a short period of time, come closer to death than ever before, yet I remained a paraplegic who would continue to defy calamity irrespective of the odds.

Twenty-four

From Hospital
To Italy To Home

T HE microbiologist rather than the surgeon became the lead
arbiter regarding medical decisions as related to the systemic
infection that remained within me. I had sepsis that was stabilising
but ongoing.

While in the Mater, many different types of doctor appeared
at the foot of my bed; an infectious diseases expert ruled out TB,
a haematologist determined I had very elevated platelets and was
in danger of clotting. This posed a small difficulty as warfarin, the
first choice blood thinner, could not be used given my reactive
history to it while in rehab back in 2002. So an alternative was
chosen.

Blood treatment and pharmaceuticals had become a concern
of mine during that stay in the Mater. While there I received a total
blood transfusion and soon after received two units of iron
enriched O negative blood. Unfortunately neither treatment
helped the sepsis and the red cells containing oxygenated blood,
remained significantly low. However I was deemed stable enough
to be transported back to Cappagh Hospital.

The person in charge of my care was a scientist not a doctor
and as such experimentation had been an inherent work method
for her. The decision to give me an IV antibiotic, known as 'Tigisil,'
a very expensive and powerful drug, was hers. She was convinced
from her lab work that the various bacteria in my system would
be beaten by this newly available drug to the Irish market. It
became apparent that sepsis was under control while I was being
treated with the drug, however the microbiologist was interested
in seeing how my system managed the sepsis without the

assistance of the drug. By April 2009 she gave me permission to take a holiday in Italy for one week – without medication.

The break from hospital life was a very welcome one even though my energy levels were very low. The arrangement with Cappagh was that I would go back into the hospital on the day of my return from Italy. With my parents I went directly from the airport to the hospital.

I was not feeling well. In fact within a day of returning, the sepsis started to significantly flare up. The microbiologist had her answer – the system was not ready to cope on its own. This 'experiment' also answered two other questions regarding dosage and duration; it was decided to maximise the dosage and extend indefinitely the duration of treatment.

On August 26, 2009 I returned home. Initially, a community nurse came twice daily to train me in administering the antibiotic. It had to be diluted a certain amount before use. Once the dilution was complete I would use a syringe to inject the fluid into a line where it directly entered the blood stream. After about five days my training was complete and I continued to inject myself twice each day until December.

During that time I returned to work, restarted physio and managed to completely avoid hospitals. In fact my next hospital admission was not until January 2011. By then it had been just over 12 months without being an in-patient, a first for me since April 2008.

Twenty-five

Old Concerns
Re-emerge

I AM the eldest of three sons. One brother lives in Italy, the other in Ireland and, together with my parents, we bought a house in Italy. We did so for a number of reasons, chief amongst them to have a place of our own while visiting my brother who is married to an Italian and now resides in Verona.

Just after Christmas for about a two-week period is our preferred time for a winter visit. It was after such a visit in mid-January 2011 that I noticed a severe swelling in my left leg around the groin and hip.

In addition to the swelling, I was feeling unwell and had little desire to eat. After a phone-call to the GP it was decided to ring an ambulance to get me admitted to Tallaght Hospital. Once assessed in A&E, admission soon followed and I was put in the care of an endocrinologist, the suspicion being there could have been some glandular involvement.

Within 24 hours of admission scans were taken and I met my consultant. He happened to grow up around the corner from where I grew up and we recognised each other. After the informal catch-up chat the more serious discussion began. He asked me had I been feeling tired lately and I answered no more than usual. Then he told me he had my scan reviewed by three different radiologists and got differing opinions on what was causing my leg to swell. Two believed it was caused by a mass or tumour, the third was not convinced that that was the case but remained unsure about the cause. He said an exploratory operation was needed to determine the cause. I said I would like to talk to my orthopaedic consultant for his view and refer back afterwards. Soon after leaving Tallaght

Hospital, with the swelling still noticeable but other symptoms gone, I met with my orthopaedic surgeon.

He took one look and told me it was bursitis, localised fluid retention, as a consequence of unhealthy scar tissue. This was a legacy of an accumulated amount of previous surgeries to that area. The swelling reduced over time, but then after another visit to Italy, I began to feel unwell once again. On this occasion a return of the known sepsis symptoms were very apparent, that is, pyrexia (temperature), tachycardia (racing heart beat), dyspnoea (shortness of breath) and rigors (shivering).

In June 2011, I was admitted to the Mater Hospital. Given previous experience I asked to be put on Tigisil, it being the antibiotic that proved useful before. After hearing my medical history, the A&E doctors decided to administer the drug. During the night I was transferred from A&E to a ward. The next day the microbiologist came to me to discuss treatment and medication. The conversation went along the following lines:

'Hi, you are back again,' he said.

'Yes with the same problem,' I responded.

'I have reviewed the blood results and the infection is not as bad this time around.'

'Good, so the Tigisil will do the trick.'

'No and that is what I wanted to talk to you about.'

'Ok.'

'Since I last saw you I discussed your case at an international conference of microbiologists. I did so because I thought this day would come.'

'What makes this day different to the past?'

'Your body has become immune to the Tigisil and it will no longer be of benefit. Knowing this could happen I needed an alternative antibiotic. However I knew no other. So I presented your case internationally outlining the four bacteria that have combined in your blood since November 2008. Thankfully that process did produce an alternative.'

'Right, will it be an intravenous or oral antibiotic?'

'It is called Fosfomycin, it's commercial name is Monuril. It should destroy three of the four bacteria in your system, the fourth you may have to tolerate. I say should destroy three of the four but I can not promise that it will – simply because stronger strains of the original bacteria are now likely to be present due to their long term coalescing. It is an oral antibiotic.'

'What will the dosage be and how often will I need to administer it?'

'It comes as a concentrated powder in two sachets at three grams per sachet. You will need to dissolve the powder in water and swallow twice daily.'

'Ok, so 3 grams or 3,000 milligrams twice per day for how long?'

'Well for the long term, quite possibly years, but essentially the duration is open ended.'

'Is there anything else I need to know before I begin?'

'Yes, it is the only remaining antibiotic left open to you. It needs to work; without it, the sepsis will in time overpower your system.'

'Meaning if it does not work. Then I will die.'

'Yes, but it is similar to when I first saw you in the spinal unit. Only then there was the option of the Tigisil. That is no longer the case.'

Then one day a breakthrough. I could stand in the leg braces without any extra support.

Twenty-six

An Outstanding Moment

DESPITE the return of the sepsis, my physio was progressing. I had a routine going that had become firmly established over the years, that is, I would return from work, enjoy lunch and then have physio in the afternoons.

At that time the physio session consisted of three sections. The first was about warming up and loosening out. Once the loosening and warming up was completed I would put on my leg braces, transfer to the chair and wheel out of the kitchen to the parallel bars in the hall. Using the bars to launch myself into an upright position, from there I would insert my hands into the crutches and begin a maximum of six laps around the kitchen table (a distance of c50m). Once completed I would transfer back into the chair and return to the kitchen for the final phase of the session, that being, the leg press weights machine.

In time I had managed to push a third of my body weight. I had shoes attached to the metal plate so the feet would remain in a fixed position allowing me to push. This leg press section of physio lasted about 10 minutes. This format to the physio remained mostly unchanged over the months and years, except for one feature.

At the end of the six laps around the kitchen table, I would practise standing in the leg braces while using the bars in front of me to balance. Over time, I became less dependent on the bars for balance. Then one day a breakthrough. I could stand in the leg braces without any extra support. I was standing upright with only the braces securing my knees while my hips held me in the vertical position. My hips, my supposed moribund hips riddled with disease were supporting my body for the first time in nine years. The moment was videoed so when I next visited the consultant he could see for himself.

A consult with the surgeon was scheduled for a month after I left the hospital. My parents were a constant support in all my activities and accompanied me to the appointment. During the discussion he made it clear that I would need to stay on the fosfomycin for the long term to quell the sepsis – something that the microbiologist had also clarified.

He also repeated the hope that all traces of the sepsis would be gone before the body became immune to the drug. Then he made reference to the possibility of an operation should the pharmacological intervention fail. He didn't provide much detail at that time about the radical nature of the procedure though within a year' such details would be discussed in a very open and explicit way.

Not withstanding this procedure, the 'outstanding' moment as captured on video was about to be shown to someone outside the family for the first time. The consultant stood over my shoulder as I took out the phone and started the video clip.

'What am I looking for?' he asked politely.

'Just keep your eyes on my hands...'

At this point in the video I was standing in the leg braces with hands out in front and fingers touching the bars.

He watched as hands were removed and one arm raised above my head with the second soon to follow. I could not see his face but my mother could. She told me afterwards that there was genuine amazement in his facial expression. As he looked on until the clip ended some two minutes later little was said.

The man returned to his seat and congratulated me on the progress. Something had shifted, his prognosis was no longer fixed in the one position. No longer was he convinced his patient would be wheelchair bound for the rest of his life. For the second time in nine years a doctor saw beyond the perceived constraints of paraplegia.

Twenty-seven

A Healing Friend And Another Hospital Visit

A COLLEAGUE made a suggestion during the course of a normal day's work. She asked had I ever been to a healer. My short answer was that I had not. I'd received blessings from priests at different times but had not met someone with recognised healing hands. She told me a meeting could be set up if I wanted it. About a week after the initial suggestion was made I decided it would do no harm to meet this man.

The healer arrived at the house one Saturday evening. We had a chat and during the course of the conversation he laid his hands on me. I was sceptical and had very low expectations. However that first touch changed my view. Heat radiated throughout my body emanating from the contact with the healing hands.

This healer has what I would describe as a deeply abiding faith. A true believer that God has an individual plan for each individual. Perhaps as a healer it is unsurprising that he has an acute medical intuition with an uncanny accuracy regarding medical issues and decisions. It is with great pride that I now describe this person as a friend.

The twice daily doses of fosfomycin continued unabated throughout 2012 but the medication was not sufficient to prevent a reoccurrence of sepsis. During the second week of September I was admitted again to the Mater Hospital.

The four horsemen of the apocalypse – otherwise known as rapid heart rate, shortness of breath, soaring temperature and shivering – returned with renewed vigour. The microbiologist repeated her view that the current antibiotic was the last available form of pharmaceutical treatment and like Tigisil, its forerunner, had its limitations.

'Could you not increase the dosage?' I wondered.

'No it would be dangerous to do so. The current dosage like all dosages is decided by a combination of body weight, age and to some extent, gender.'

'It just appears as if it is beginning to lose its effectiveness.'

'As with all drug treatments if taken in the long term, the body becomes immune to them.'

'Have I become immune to the fosfomycin?'

'It is too soon to be completely sure but if the frequency and intensity of septic flare-ups continue then yes your system has immunised itself against the treatment.'

'Is the current level of infection greater or less than June of last year or than when it initially occurred in November 2009.'

'It is not as severe now as previously.'

'But it could become as bad or worse than before particularly if my system rejects the antibiotic.'

'Yes and given that you have currently been taking fosfomycin for 15 months, it is conceivable that that could now be starting to happen. Though as I say it is difficult to be definitive at this juncture. There is an orthopaedic procedure that could be appropriate but it is a discussion best left to the surgeons. It is called a gurdle operation, though for you it probably would not be overly appealing.'

At this point my mind started to wonder if there was a beneficial procedure available to me why had it not come up for discussion before now? It soon became apparent as to why this was so.

The Mater Hospital in September of 2012 had a system of a medical consultant assigned to each ward with each patient also having his or her own specialist consultant. This could be an orthopaedic consultant or whatever form of specialist consultant most appropriate to the individual patient. The general consultant made his rounds on a daily basis, usually in the early morning. One morning he came round with his team of doctors and told me directly: 'We have a problem with you.'

'What is it?'

'Well, you can stand.'

'I'm sorry, why should that be problematic?'

'The osteomylitis in your hip is well established and proving difficult to eradicate via antibiotics alone. So at this point, consideration has to be given to an operation for its removal. Such an operation would compromise your ability to stand up.'

'So what your saying is the sepsis associated with the osteomylitis is now threatening my life and the appropriate response is radical surgery that will confine me to a wheelchair without hope of ever getting out of it irrespective of any physiotherapy.'

'That's about it. I am not an orthopaedic specialist, therefore, I would not be involved directly but your consultant will be around later today.'

Needless to say that particular conversation caused me to reflect like I had not done since the initial injury 10 years earlier. Only on this occasion the question in need of answering focused not only on adapting to a different life but on living or dying. My surgeon arrived at the foot of my bed that afternoon. He re-affirmed what the senior doctor had said that morning. Only he went into greater detail about just what a gurdle operation entails.

'It is the removal of the infected bone from your body. In your case the left hip would be removed as would about 50 per cent of your femur bone. The infected bone would be replaced by a metal alternative. This substitute metal however would undermine skeletal support for any vertical weight bearing. In other words sitting and lying would be fine but standing would not be.'

'You have seen me stand up. I do not want to throw that away under any circumstances.'

'I would not ask you to, only where I thought your life was in danger.'

'And you think we have reached that point now.'

'Not yet but it seems that time is coming.'

'Are there any other alternatives?'

'I have discussed your case at the weekly hospital open forum. It provides an opportunity to share views and reasoning with other surgical consultants. Various opinions were expressed; prominent amongst them was life trumps mobility. The patient once fully informed and of sound mind as it were should be the final arbiter not the surgeon and finally it was suggested nothing should be done at this time. Do not precipitate an action prior to it becoming an absolute imperative.'

'I do not believe immediate surgery is needed to save my life.'

'No, it is not. The infection markers within your blood are beginning to settle down. In fact I would say all things being equal you could return home next week, if you feel up to it, there is no rush.'

I returned home within a few days knowing that I had committed to a course of inaction for now in the fervent hope that this recent flare-up proved was an exception and not the rule.

Twenty-eight

A New Doctor

A CONSULTATION was arranged with my surgeon for late October 2012. He told me he no longer wanted to operate on my left hip. His view was it would likely need further surgery, pointedly so, given the stubborn nature of the osteomylitis. Osteomylitis is an infection of the bone and very difficult to treat with antibiotics because the bone acts as a shield against medication. It reduces the effectiveness of the treatment because the antibiotics are not designed to penetrate bone.

Ironically, it is when a sepsis flare-up occurs and the infection gets into the blood that the drugs are at their most effective because the infection is no longer shielded by the bone. Since leaving the hospital a two part question had dominated my thoughts; would I rather die from infection or live wheelchair bound for the rest of my days? This was the same question the surgeon asked that October – a hypothetical question, yet one tinged with more than a hint of realism.

'You know I'm sworn to uphold, maintain and protect life – no matter what the circumstances might be.'

'Yes I understand but I need you to understand I would rather die from sepsis than live without any possibility of walking again. It's a position that goes against every fibre of your being – I'm sure.'

'It is.'

'Well where can we go from here?'

'I would like to refer you to another consultant with a widely recognised reputation for treating infected joints. I would not have the same level of experience as him.'

'Ok.'

'Right, I will send him a letter outlining your history and ask him to see if I have missed anything.'

The new surgeon saw me within a week. He took on board what my previous consultant advised in his letter and expressed a desire to explore my left hip with an MRI scan. He then wanted to discuss my case at a surgical forum held occasionally in Cappagh Hospital.

On November 14, I was admitted for an MRI and asked to join the forum to be held that evening in a lecture theatre of the hospital. The scan provided good news as it could not detect any osteomylitis. However pooling – the process where fluid gathers or collects in an area it should not – was evident.

Excess or foreign fluid is a fertile location for bacterial infection. Given the possibility of an infection it was decided to aspirate the hip. An aspiration is where a big bore needle is inserted into an area and sample fluid/tissue is withdrawn for testing purposes. The result of the aspiration was as good as the MRI result, all clear.

The open surgical forum that evening was new to me, I had never appeared at a lectern facing a lecture theatre full of surgeons before. Many questions were put to me but two from the same person stood out: 'If we were to operate with a 50:50 chance of success, would you want to go ahead?'

'By success do you mean I would retain my current ability to stand assisted by crutches and leg braces?'

'Yes, whatever you have now you would retain.'

'Then I would want it, yes.'

'If there was only a 10 per cent chance of success, would you want the operation?'

'No.'

Perhaps the surgeon who asked those questions did so deliberately to provoke me into thinking about new surgical options now that the osteomylitis was no longer evident in my hip. Whether that was the intention or not I will never know. Yet the possibility of constructive surgery to assist my physiotherapy was something that captured my attention.

Twenty-nine

The Possibility Of Historic Surgery

EVERY year since I left the National Rehabilitation Hospital, in 2002, I have returned annually for a KUB, (Kidney, Urether and Bladder) check-up. It was made clear at the end of my rehab that the kidneys were the organs that suffer the most when sitting for a long period of time. That is why standing up every day has a great medical significance for all paralytics.

However, even with standing up between the bars or on crutches incorporated into my daily physiotherapy routine, kidney difficulties continue to arise. By December 2012, another kidney stone had to be removed, its location, on this occasion was the urethra – the tube linking the kidney and the bladder. Subsequent to its removal the urologist informed me that my right kidney, if functioning at all, was doing so at a diminished level. Fortunately the other kidney was compensating for this lack of functionality and displayed all the requisite signs of a healthy organ.

The striking feature of 2013 was the resumption of everyday life without a necessary stay in hospital, it was akin to 2010. The osteomylitis had gone, the associated sepsis had gone, the daily dosage of fosfomycin continued while the balance between work and physio remained stable throughout that year. In September, I had an appointment to see the surgeon in Cappagh Hospital; it was an opportunity to make a request.

He greeted me warmly.

'Good to see you again. You are looking well. Any flare-ups since last year?'

'None at all I have been balancing work and physio without complaints.'

'Continuing with the daily antibiotic?'

'Yes, that is what has got me healthy and is probably keeping me so but I have a request.'

'Ok, let's hear it.'

'I would like a hip replacement since I am free of infection and now would be a good time to do it.'

'Well your left hip is not 100 per cent structurally sound with the cartilage absent, the bone fragmented and the joint anatomically abnormal. But why would you want more surgery when you may not get the most out of a hip replacement when you are wheelchair bound?'

'I would want it to benefit my drive to get out of the chair and not to be dependent on it forever and a day.'

'So you are fully determined to leave the chair behind you one day.'

'Yes I have been from day one.'

'Ok, but you should know to the best of my knowledge a total hip replacement in a paraplegic is rare. I'm not even sure that it has ever been done before in this country.'

'Listen, it's a chance to make a little history I have no difficulty becoming – patient zero. When you make a success of it others will follow the example you laid down. Establishing precedence is the essence of a patient zero case study.'

'I would like to carry out the operation here in this hospital. It is an operation I would carry out with a partner surgeon. He would provide you with the plastic cup or the artificial socket part of the new joint while I would provide the ball part, that is, a metallic head to your femur that would fit inside the new socket.'

'Great, any idea when it can go ahead.'

'I need to talk to my colleague first and arrange a mutually acceptable time but the hospital should be in touch. My best guess would be November.'

'Thanks...'

I did see the surgeon in November but the surgery was suspended for another time. It was a Monday afternoon in late November and I had been waiting in the ward of the hospital as my surgeon finished his morning list of procedures. He arrived with his colleague at about 2.30pm obviously direct from theatre since both had their surgical scrubs on.

What followed was a difficult conversation. My surgeon approached about 10 yards ahead of his colleague and in a lowered voice he said: 'We may have a problem with the cup.'

'What's the problem?'

'We'll talk about it now with my colleague.'

After a short introduction, the colleague outlined his position. 'You have a long history with sepsis.'

'I have had bouts of it for the last five years, however the most recent MRI showed no osteomylitis which is a prime indicator of sepsis. If I am to be honest my left hip has not been right since an initial infection in 2002.'

'What happened then?'

'Well I had bleeding into the bone.'

'And what caused that?'

'I was on anti-coagulant and it was surmised that heavy physiotherapy precipitated bleeding.'

'Why were you on the anti-coagulant and what was its name?'

'I developed a clot in my left leg and Warfarin was used to break it up.'

'Was it your one and only clot or were there others?'

'I had one previously many years ago in the same area.'

'Ok. I do not think this operation is the right thing to do. You have a history of clotting something that can reoccur with this operation and in a post operative context clots are a primary concern even in patients without your history. Secondly, the sepsis, are you still taking fosfomycin?'

'Yes at 6,000mg per day, I dissolve the powdered sachets with water and administer twice a day 3,000mg at a time.'

'That there is another reason why it would be unwise to proceed.'

'What do you mean exactly?'

'Well aside from the inevitable immunity your body will develop to the treatment. We have no idea how your system can manage without the medication. Has the fosfomycin masked the sepsis or eradicated it? Aside from the clotting and the status of the sepsis there is another overriding concern.'

'That being?'

'The questionable benefit a hip replacement will be to a paraplegic.'

'Well, I would not share that concern given that I have had neurological return for quite sometime now. I am specifically referring to the reflexes returning to the soles of my feet some years ago.'

'Despite that I still remain unconvinced about the procedure.'

'What do you require to change your point of view aside from a clear MRI and returned reflexes?'

At this point, my consultant made a suggestion.

'What if Ciarán stops the antibiotic for say a month and comes back then for a review by the pre-assessment clinic.'

'I'm very busy up to January and would prefer three months off the antibiotic prior to pre-assessment.'

The conversation with the 'cup' man frustrated me but on reflection it was always likely that another doctor would follow the medical approach already in play since January 2002. A conservative approach where one fact clouds medical thinking. In short, the paraplegia has left this man in a wheelchair and a hip replacement will do nothing to change that reality.

Needless to say that emphasis or approach did not have my support. I knew full sensation and movement had returned to my hips. I also knew to fulfil the latent potential of my hips barriers to progress needed to be removed, namely arthritis and osteomylitis. Surgical removal of those barriers which provided renewed pelvic stability became my focus.

Although I was told to stop the antibiotic it was difficult to do so. For the most part it served me well with only one septic flare-up throughout the 29 months of use. Had my system become dependent on it and if so how could I manage without it? Knowing its termination had become a prerequisite to the surgery I slowly reduced my intake of the antibiotic and by Christmas I had stopped taking it altogether.

The operation was deemed a success; it took about three hours to complete or twice the usual duration.

Thirty

The Surgery

I N early February, I received a call to attend the pre-assessment clinic in Cappagh. Patients with known pre-existing medical conditions are asked to attend prior to an operation being carried out. It involves a very comprehensive assessment of the patient's orthopaedic and general medical history, as well as a check on blood pressure and heart beat, while blood and urine samples are also taken for analysis.

Prior to the paralysis, I had undergone an operation in 1991 for a partial fusion of the L3 and L4 vertebrae. A surgical response to a spinal congenital condition was deemed appropriate. It was the first general anaesthetic, (GA), I had ever received, by 2015, this figure had increased to over a dozen GAs for various reasons mostly orthopaedic in nature.

Within a week of the assessment official notification of the procedure was sent on by post. I would be admitted on the morning of February 24 for a total left hip replacement that afternoon. After the admission process was completed I had a chance to talk with my consultant;

'Good morning. I have a light list today simply to give ample time to yourself.'

'So am I last on your surgical list today?'

'Yes. Normally this procedure would take 90 minutes but your situation requires further attention due to the abnormal anatomy.'

'Specifically due to the joint degradation and potential infection.'

'Plus the insertion of the plastic cup not being straight forward will take longer than usual.'

'Are you confident the hip will not dislocate? Speaking to my rehabilitation doctor dislocation would seem to be a primary concern.'

'I am less concerned about dislocation than I am about bleeding. I have decided to insert a tripolarisation hip.'

'What does that mean?'

'It means that the joint will be anchored to bone in three areas. Most new hips are bipolarised, with just the two anchors. The extra anchor decreases the likelihood of a dislocation. In addition, the actual scale of the metal joint decreases further the possibility of dislocation. What remains of the head of your femur will be removed and the base of the joint inserted into the long section of the bone.'

'What is the length of the new joint from end to end?'

'About 25cms or 10 inches long.'

'Why would bleeding concern you?'

'The nature of the surgery is deeply invasive. The objective is to establish a union between man-made material and body tissue. Something that cannot be achieved without blood loss, remember surgery is a controlled trauma deliberately inflicted on the body. The incision will be along the side of the leg.'

The operation was deemed a success; it took about three hours to complete or twice the usual duration. It involved two surgeons though at one stage a third, the professor and head of surgery, was invited to share his view. Blood loss proved to be within expected limits and not a concern. Immediately after the procedure, I was admitted to the high dependence unit, HDU, for about 48 hours.

In HDU, a patient's vital signs are constantly monitored by assigned nurses, where the ratio between nurse and patient is one to one. I remained in bed for the next 10 days as a precaution against infection before mobilisation. Thankfully none ensued and physiotherapy resumed within a fortnight of the operation.

Thirty-one

Patient Zero

A FEW months after leaving the orthopaedic hospital I attended my annual assessment at the National Rehabilitation Hospital. The usual rehab consultant was away on maternity leave and in her place was someone I had known while in rehab after my injury. This someone happened to be the former head of spinal rehabilitation and had a professional association with the hospital for many decades. She remembered me and we recalled some of the characters, both patients and staff, from that time. Then the conversation turned to health matters.

'You have had a hip replacement. How have you been feeling since then? Any flare-ups in the sepsis.'

'Good. No flare-ups at all.'

'Should the sepsis return it would be very serious in that it would co-mingle with the titanium leading to metal poisoning.'

'I was warned about that but fortunately I feel fine.'

'Did your consultant refer to the rarity of a hip replacement in a paraplegic?'

'He did say it was unusual. So how often has it happened before?'

'Well you are the first paraplegic I have come across in all my time associated with rehabilitation medicine to have the procedure.'

'I mentioned the phrase patient zero to the surgeon at one point but I think he was more focused on a positive surgical outcome than any notoriety.'

'And rightly so but what interests me is the prospect of changing medical assumptions about the way spinal patients receive orthopaedic treatment. Specifically, your case could set the medical precedent required for earlier orthopaedic intervention with arthritic hip joints whatever about infected lower limb joints in general.'

'Well perhaps in time orthopaedic precedent will be set I would like that to be the case. I know from a microbiological perspective mine is a curious case. Given the rarity of the bacterial mix that formed my type of sepsis and my recovery to date it's likely that at some point in the future antigens from my blood will be analysed closely.'

'Sounds like another first.'

'Well maybe so but of all the possible medical precedents that may arise, it is the physiotherapy legacy that interests me as much as any other.'

At that time, my physiotherapy had improved noticeably from the time before the operation. Before the operation I could no longer walk with the braces and crutches round and round the kitchen table. This had to stop due to the pain in my hips although I did manage to stand between the parallel bars in the hall-way of the house.

So while the state of my hips had curtailed the physio, their state did not stop it altogether yet this lower intensity physio provided the foundation upon which I could improve. The maximum distance covered before the operation was 50m per session with the leg braces and crutches. This improved to 100m per session x 2 daily.

When weights and electric pads sessions are added to the two assisted walks, four hours of physio Monday through to Thursday became the norm. I would not stop at the weekends either though tapered down activity prevailed on Saturdays and Sundays. All told 20 hours of physio per week had become the norm.

I have mentioned my physio habits and workload more than once primarily because it is my response to my condition. Certainly the hope would be that 'incomplete' spinal patients would follow my example particularly when it becomes clear that return of limb functionality and other bodily functions are the outcome of the hard work. More important is to show utter respect for each individual's set of personal circumstances, their state of mind and the decisions emanating from that context.

Thirty-two

The Second Hip Replacement

THE meeting with the rehabilitation consultant occurred about a week before my next orthopaedic consultation.

'How are you?'

'Going well. You've seen the X-ray of the hip. It's been four months since the operation how does it appear to you?'

'Nothing untoward I'm happy to say. At this point the soft tissue surrounding the new hip will be anchoring it so that it becomes completely embedded into position.'

'The physio has improved in terms of both strength and endurance. But I have another request, would you consider replacing my other hip?'

'Yes, I will do that. To some extent it is completing the job. While each one of us has two hips they act together as one system. So to repair the system both hips need correcting.'

'Where would you like to do it? I know you work in a number of hospitals.'

'I would like to do it here. It is the best option for the procedure but I have to tell you it will be sometime before you will be admitted.'

'Any idea of timescale?'

'Well it could be the new year.'

'Could you do it sooner in another hospital?'

'Yes, but this is the only hospital I share privilege to practise with the surgeon who inserts the plastic cups that hold the metal in place. I could do that part of the procedure as well but I am out of practise, whereas my colleague does it routinely.'

'The same man you worked with on my left hip?'

'Yes.'

'Ok and presumably at some point I will get notice of the admission in the post.'

'I will put you on my waiting list today but as I said it could be the New Year, with luck maybe before Christmas.'

As it turned out, March 2, 2015 was both the day of admission and the day of the procedure. Upon arrival just after seven o'clock on a cold, frosty morning, my overwhelming feeling was one of joy. At last the arthritic hips once referred to as more appropriate to a 65-year-old than a 35-year-old, were being completely replaced with the best metal joints available. The admission process was an exact replica of the previous year even down to the few words I had with the surgeon. Similarity in both approach and surgical technique was sought and subsequently attained by himself and the 'cup' man.

Two days after the operation I returned from the high dependence unit and was put in St. Paul's Ward. I soon needed to evacuate my bowel. It proved to be a long experience as my insides seemed to have turned to liquid and diarrhoea made its presence felt.

Having eventually ended my toilet toils, I returned to bed but sleep proved elusive due to extensive cramping. A sample was taken for analysis after three episodes in a row. It proved to be negative for the various bacteria that can cause such explosive episodes yet both the diarrhoea and cramping continued for over 20 days. Doctor after doctor reassured me it would go away on its own.

By March 9 I had been moved to room six on the ward and it was at this time that a pressure sore developed around my sacrum. Two weeks later sepsis had set in and once again I had become seriously sick.

At the beginning of March I was infection free, my haemoglobin was a healthy 14.4, my skin was unbroken and my weight was 85kgs. Three weeks later sepsis had set in, haemoglobin, (iron containing oxygen found in the blood's red cells) had dropped to less than 8.0, a pressure sore later categorised at the highest level of severity ravaged my sacrum and I weighed 75kgs – a drop of 10kgs or 22lbs in 22 days.

Once the sepsis set in, the doctors started to refer to the diarrhoea as a symptom. That riled me as the diarrhoea on day 22 was a symptom as it was on day 1, yet the medical consensus for a three-week period was that it would go away on its own – clearly a false view. While the diarrhoea dissipated, the sepsis and the pressure sore worsened to the extent that a long stay in hospital was inevitable.

*He did not endear himself
to me with his approach yet he
outlined a sequence of events
that would in time become
the focus of my attention.*

Thirty-three

Pressure Sore

AFTER a three-week period of treatment, the sepsis was in abeyance and the decision was made to attend a plastics consultant. Cappagh is an orthopaedic hospital and does not have practising plastic surgeons on campus. Connolly Hospital 20 minutes away by taxi is a general hospital and has a plastics department, which is where I met the plastics specialist. It proved to be both abrupt and dismissive in nature.

After waiting for about two hours the specialist arrived in the small windowless room, where I was waiting on a plinth with my sacrum exposed for inspection. After taking a look he spoke; 'When did this first show itself?'

The question was directed to the nurse accompanying me that day.

'About a month ago.'

'I do not understand why this was not operated on before now.'

'Well the team were interested in a plastics view before any decisions were made.'

'My view is a flap procedure would be appropriate, colostomy bag and lying prone for about six weeks followed by a recovery period of six months or so. I will let my colleague know; no doubt he will be in contact anyway.'

With that he was gone and during the course of the four-minute interaction he did not direct his words to me at all and barely allowed the nurse a word in edgeways. Needless to say, he did not endear himself to me with his approach yet he outlined a sequence of events that would in time become the focus of my attention.

As a recipient of a flap procedure before, I was not inclined to accept another. For me history was repeating itself, only this time the benefit of previous experience and specifically the knowledge gained as a consequence of that experience would guide me.

The first decision made after my return to Cappagh was to tell the orthopaedic consultant that I would not be choosing to have a flap procedure. Since the flap operation did not constitute a medical imperative, the life of the patient was not at risk so the decision could come within the purview of the patient.

Manuka honey usually imported from New Zealand has strong healing qualities. So much so that pharmaceutical companies are producing Manuka-based products for the treatment of soft tissue ulcers and sores. Such products were used in the form of a poultice to dress the sore every two days or so. The initial dimensions of the pressure sore were sizeable. A diameter of a tennis ball together with half a diameter of another tennis ball would roughly be the size of the crater residing in my backside.

Not only could nurses place their closed fists into it, the cavity had joined with a sinus (a gap in the flesh), to penetrate the flesh completely exposing the bone. The sinus was an artefact from the previous year's hip replacement. When a wound or sore is so deep as to expose bone it is categorised as a level four class wound. There are no level five class wounds. Given this context, keeping the site clean and free of infection was both challenging and necessary.

Sometime before the sepsis settled down I got another bout of diarrhoea. In addition I had also acquired MRSA, an antibiotic resistant infection, which can slow healing of wounds and or cause systemic illness. Knowing that the primary bout led to a septic reaction, I was determined that on this occasion it would be treated properly.

I sought out a doctor I had known from previous visits to the hospital who had since attained consultant status.

She explained that it was highly likely that the diarrhoea would have been viral in nature, especially considering its presence at a time when very strong antibiotics were being administered to destroy bacteria throughout the body.

Furthermore, she ruled out irritable bowel syndrome on the basis that waking up to a soiled bed removed any psychological aspect to the infection. Being viral in nature it would have to work its way through the system. However on this occasion unlike before, there would be no stomach acid reduction medication. This, plus dietary advice, limited the duration of the diarrhoea to just under a week. That was a big improvement on the previous three-week stint and this time my weight remained stable.

Throughout the illness and with the exception of about two weeks, physiotherapy continued improving. In late March, I was covering a distance of about 20m with braces and crutches, and by July the distance covered was 200m. During August and into September another milestone was reached – walking with braces and crutches for a quarter of a kilometre per session. While the progress was palpable my sense of joy was constrained not by the sense of achievement but by the less than healthy state of my sacrum.

The shoes I wore for physiotherapy had lasted since 2002 but after 13 years they were coming apart, a new pair was required. Cappagh Hospital has a fine orthotics department and an appointment was set up where measurements were taken to provide new customised shoes. The orthotist had a Dutch accent but spoke perfect English: 'On your chart I have paraplegia and shoes. I need more information.'

A newborn, particularly when you are a direct relative, is precious and instantly loveable.

Thirty-four

Seven Months
And Counting

OCTOBER 2 marked the start of my eighth straight month in hospital. It was only the second time I left the hospital throughout that time. Unlike the first time when I went from hospital to hospital and back again, this was altogether different. On October 2, 1965, my parents got married, 50 years later they decided to renew their vows and celebrate afterwards.

It was a special occasion for another reason as well – a grandchild, a first for my parents; and a niece, a first for me and a first for my younger brother and his wife. A woman of rare generosity and sharp insightfulness. Little Fia, was born July 15 while I was in the hospital. We had never met, so naturally the excitement was high.

In truth, I always found it difficult to understand how people could get so caught up in photos and videos of newborns. After all, a baby is just a baby. How wrong I was. A newborn, particularly when you are a direct relative, is precious and instantly loveable. Another reason for a great evening (though definitely more mundane) was the non-hospital food. To say I gorged on a wide variety of food would be to understate my behaviour – it was closer to gluttony.

A week later brought another trip beyond the confines of the hospital. Back to Connolly Hospital for a second plastics consultation, only on this occasion with a colleague of the previous man. The conversation was revealing:

'When did you get your infection?'

'Well, I had sepsis as a consequence of a pressure sore.'

'That is not what I mean.'

'Well it was not a localised infection it was systemic, it was carried by the blood throughout the body.'

'No. It's a common misconception to think that pressure sores are caused by pressure; they are not, infection caused your sore nothing else.'

'I had diarrhoea before the sore developed.'

'That was the cause of your sore.'

'Until today I had my suspicions but you are the first doctor to confirm them.'

'From the photographs and the oral history to date, I would categorise your sore a three to four level wound. Probably closer to a four, level four occurs when bone is exposed and is therefore the deepest a soft tissue wound can be.'

After a close look at the wound he said: What is important here is the natural healing. It takes the lead and an operation should only be considered as supplemental to that natural process.'

'Do you think an operation is appropriate at this time?'

'Looking at it now, I would not think so. In fact, the healing is what I would expect to see from a person without paralysis rather than a paraplegic. When did you notice your neurological return?'

'When the reflexes returned to the soles of my feet.'

With that, he said very little else but his facial expression was one of genuine acceptance that he was seeing the patient as a person overcoming their condition rather than a condition overcoming the patient.

He wanted the negative pressure device or VAC to be continued at a slightly lower level than before and its attached poultice to be redressed every three to four days. I was to return for a follow-up consult six weeks later when he would assess the progress and discuss the possibility of a flap operation at that time.

The six weeks passed and I returned to the out-patients section of the plastics clinic, on October 9. Disappointingly, the consultant was absent and in his place, the registrar oversaw clinic duty. As before the dimensions of the sore were taken though the registrar's measurements showed less of an improvement than Cappagh's measurements. Irrespective the registrar said she would call the consultant to discuss her view and ask him for his opinion.

'I have spoken to the surgeon and he wants you to be mentally prepared for a discussion about a flap operation next time he sees you. He would like that to be in two weeks time. His view is that barring a radical improvement in the sore an operation would be the best course of action.'

'The recovery time will be about six months?'

'It could be but that varies from patient to patient.'

'Would I need a colostomy bag?'

'Some patients do require bags.'

'And I would be immobilised lying on my front for four to six weeks prior to putting any weight on the sacrum.'

'Yes, there has to be a period of pressure relief in order for the flap to take.'

'I have to tell you this is not my dream in life.'

'Well, give it some thought and have a full discussion with the surgeon in a fortnight.'

That meeting had not gone the way I had hoped it would go. Ideally I would have preferred the surgeon to be present instead he got his information secondhand; an out of focus photograph of the sore and dimensions that were at variance with those taken by the hospital.

Furthermore, I still felt a strong resentment to my entire situation. Were it not for a basic diagnostic error seven months beforehand I would have been home balancing a full schedule of physiotherapy with work. Instead there remained the possibility of an unwanted operation and continually diminishing time in the gym.

The number of patients in Cappagh grew rapidly as the months went by yet the number of physiotherapists remained the same. My physio time had been constrained due to the MRSA. Since late

May early June, I could go to the gym last in the day when everyone else had been seen.

This had to be the case given the health threat posed by the staph infection to other patients, in particular, post operative patients and the threat it continued to pose me. Being last on the physio list only worked when physios were available. Given their extra workload they became less able to oversee my physical therapy. In fact, the month of October contrasted greatly with the month of May. In May I had two sessions per day but by the end of October this was reduced to two sessions per week.

During the two weeks between visits to Connolly Hospital the sore continued to improve but not to the extent whereby a flap procedure became unnecessary. I had an appointment for 13.54pm at the plastics clinic, not a minute before and not a minute after. About two hours after this allotted time, I met the man I had come to see.

'Sorry about the last day I just could not be here. I was not trying to avoid you I promise.'

'I'll take your word for it.'

'It seems to be improving but you can make up your mind.'

'Yes, I would say it has decreased by about a third since I first saw it. Now is the time to operate. Remember I said the operation would be supplemental to the natural healing. Well, your healing is sufficient for me to say there is a 90 per cent chance the flap will take in time for you to be home by Christmas. I have booked your theatre time for November 19.'

'I thought it was a six-month recovery time.'

'That would be the other 10 per cent but I do think that less likely. When I saw you first, two decisions needed to be made, one by you, the other by me. Mine was to decide whether you would be a good candidate for the surgery; yours was to decide if you wanted the operation.'

'I would be prone for about four to six weeks with a colostomy bag.'

'You would be immobilised to assist the flap to take. We would have you on a sand bed where there is little or no pressure on the body in the lying position. In your case a bag is not necessary.'

'What if I did nothing, would the VAC work?'

'The VAC will help the closure of the sore. By March or April of next year it will have sealed up but the skin in that area will be weak and likely to break down in the future. However in the meantime you could go home, gauge the dos and don'ts of activities that would pressurise the sacrum and behave accordingly.'

'I am colonised by MRSA. It is present in the sore which is not helpful.'

'We will be guided by the microbiologist but it is sensitive to Vancomycin. That will be the antibiotic to combat a possible flare-up once the donor flesh seals the sore.'

'When you say the flap will 'take' do you mean total integration or union between the donor flesh and the sore?'

'Yes.'

'So no gaps or voids in the flesh, no chance of creating another bacterial hideaway like what happened before with my first flap operation.'

'Full union or integration of the flesh will occur; the only question is how long it will take. My best guess is four to six weeks.'

'You have done this operation many times before?'

'Yes and it has worked for patients with far less sensation around the sacrum than you.'

'When do you need a decision?'

'By early next week. We need to arrange for the sand bed and reserve a room.'

'Ok, I'll have a decision for you by then.' (For the record, I decided to have the operation.)

'In the meantime keep doing whatever you are doing because I have not seen such good healing around a sacral sore in quite a while.'

'Keep doing whatever you are doing.'

Actually, I did make a change. One that increased the rate of natural healing. I stopped taking sugar in tea. In early October I started to analyse my diet to see if any improvements could be made. What struck me was my excessive tea drinking.

In hospital, tea is served with breakfast, lunch and dinner as well as in the afternoons and evenings. My habit is to have sweet tea, four sachets of white sugar. With an average of four cups and 16 sachets per day, it became safe to assume my consumption of sugar was too high.

When such a level of sugar is ingested the pancreas responds in kind by upping its levels of sugar production. Once that process starts then the blood is sweetened to the extent that it no longer provides an efficient healing regime to the body. Too much sugar in the system and light headedness is apparent; too little and sweating occurs.

Thirty-five

Questions Answered

QUESTIONS that are often asked of me include: How is it possible for you to maintain a positive outlook when time and time again you are blasted by negative circumstances? Have you ever wondered 'why me?' Is it difficult?

Maintaining a positive outlook is only possible by not feeling sorry for yourself. So the question then becomes how to avoid wallowing in a swamp of self-pity? True belief, staunch determination and unwavering discipline will prevent the possibility of drowning in self-pity and together allow an individual to commit to a course of action. Thus as negative circumstances arise, the fortified immune system of belief, determination and discipline will fend off would-be emotional assaults.

I can safely say I have never asked 'why me?' Quite the opposite, in fact. I continue to ask why not me on the basis I am no different to anyone else – my life does not come with a guarantee assuring me perfect health from birth to death. No one's life does.

Finally, is it difficult?

Yes, of course it's difficult, but anything worth doing is rarely easy. I continue to heal and maintain my faith in a full recovery. On January 27, 2002, I made a decision to walk again. It happened to be my first day of paraplegia and, to this day, I dedicate my life to that decision.

At present, I am in a wheelchair. In the future, I will not be.

I do not view these paralysed years as lost; on the contrary, a conviction grows within me that I am now 14 years closer to walking away from the chair.

Epilogue

As I write this last page, it is the autumn of 2016. The New Zealand 'All Blacks' are returning to our shores to play Ireland in the Aviva.

New Zealand are world champions for several reasons – not least because of their indomitable spirit and consistent standards, each of which I too need to embody as time marches on.

Life has changed since 2002. The biggest change without doubt was becoming paralysed but I remain hopeful about the future.

That hope is grounded not on wishful thinking but physiological characteristics evident within me.

I do not view these paralysed years as lost; on the contrary, a conviction grows within me that I am now 14 years closer to walking away from the chair.

Acknowledgements

I WOULD like to thank: The CYM Terenure Sports Club, Terenure College and Terenure Rugby Club for their material and financial support, The National Rehabilitation Hospital, The Mater Hospital, Cappagh Hospital and Tallaght Hospital for their medical expertise, The IRFU Charitable Trust for the impetus and encouragement to write this book.

I'd like to thank my publisher PJ Cunningham and his wife Rosemary at Ballpoint Press for their expert advice in helping me to tell my story. Thanks also to book designer Joe Coyle, to John Scally for guiding me through the early writing and editing process, and to Ollie Campbell, a rugby legend whose encouragement was invaluable.

Finally, for their unflinching, unreserved and universal support, my parents and brothers deserve more gratitude than words can convey.